GRAPHIC HISTORY

THE LEWIS AND CLARK EXPEDITION

by Jessica Gunderson

illustrated by Steve Erwin, Keith Williams,
and Charles Barnett III

Consultant:
Gerald Newborg
Head Archivist
State Historical Society of North Dakota

Capstone
press

Mankato, Minnesota

YAJ
GRAPHIC
GRAPHICS
404 0067

Graphic Library is published by Capstone Press,
151 Good Counsel Drive, P.O. Box 669, Mankato, Minnesota 56002.
www.capstonepress.com

1 2 3 4 5 6 11 10 09 08 07 06

Library of Congress Cataloging-in-Publication Data
Gunderson, Jessica Sarah, 1976–
    The Lewis and Clark Expedition / by Jessica Gunderson.
    p. cm.—(Graphic library. Graphic history)
    Summary: "In graphic novel format, tells the dramatic story of Lewis and Clark's
exploration of the unmapped American west"—Provided by publisher.
    Includes bibliographical references and index.
    ISBN-13: 978-0-7368-6493-0 (hardcover : alk. paper)
    ISBN-10: 0-7368-6493-8 (hardcover : alk. paper)
    ISBN-13: 978-0-7368-9655-9 (softcover pbk.)
    ISBN-10: 0-7368-9655-4 (softcover pbk.)
    1. Lewis and Clark Expedition (1804–1806)—Juvenile literature. 2. West (U.S.)—
Discovery and exploration—Juvenile literature. 3. West (U.S.)—Description and travel—
Juvenile literature. 4. Lewis, Meriwether, 1774–1809—Juvenile literature. 5. Clark, William,
1770–1838—Juvenile literature. 6. Explorers—West (U.S.)—Biography—Juvenile literature. I.
Title. II. Series.
F592.7.G86 2007
917.804'2—dc22
                                                                        2006009171

Designer
Bob Lentz

Production Designer
Kim Brown

Colorist
Dan Davis

Editor
Megan Schoeneberger

Editor's note: Direct quotations from primary sources are indicated by a yellow background.

Direct quotations appear on the following pages:
Page 22 from November 24, 1805, journal entry by William Clark; Page 21 from November
7, 1805, journal entry by William Clark; as reprinted in *The Lewis and Clark Journals:
An American Epic of Discovery: The Abridgment of the Definitive Nebraska Edition*,
edited by Gary E. Moulton (Lincoln, Neb.: University of Nebraska Press, 2003).

TABLE OF CONTENTS

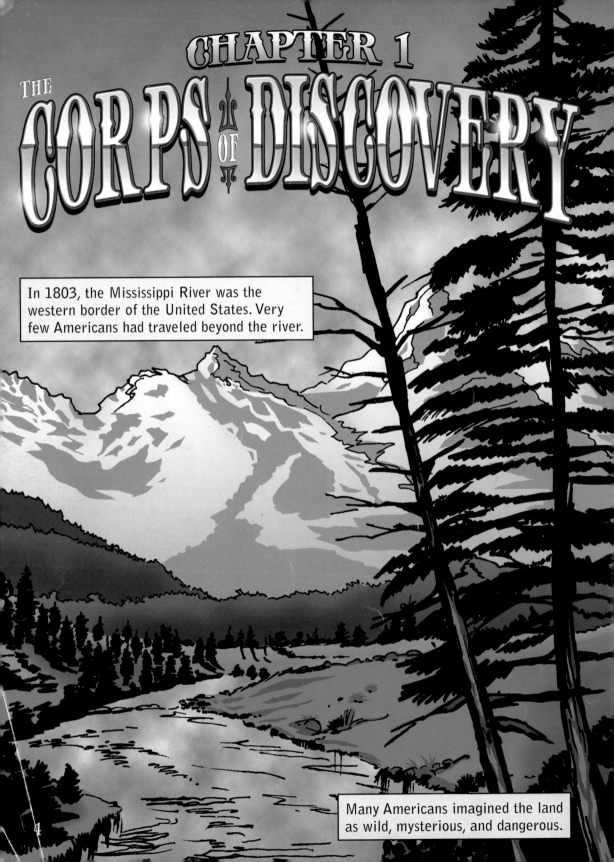

CHAPTER 1
THE CORPS OF DISCOVERY

In 1803, the Mississippi River was the western border of the United States. Very few Americans had traveled beyond the river.

Many Americans imagined the land as wild, mysterious, and dangerous.

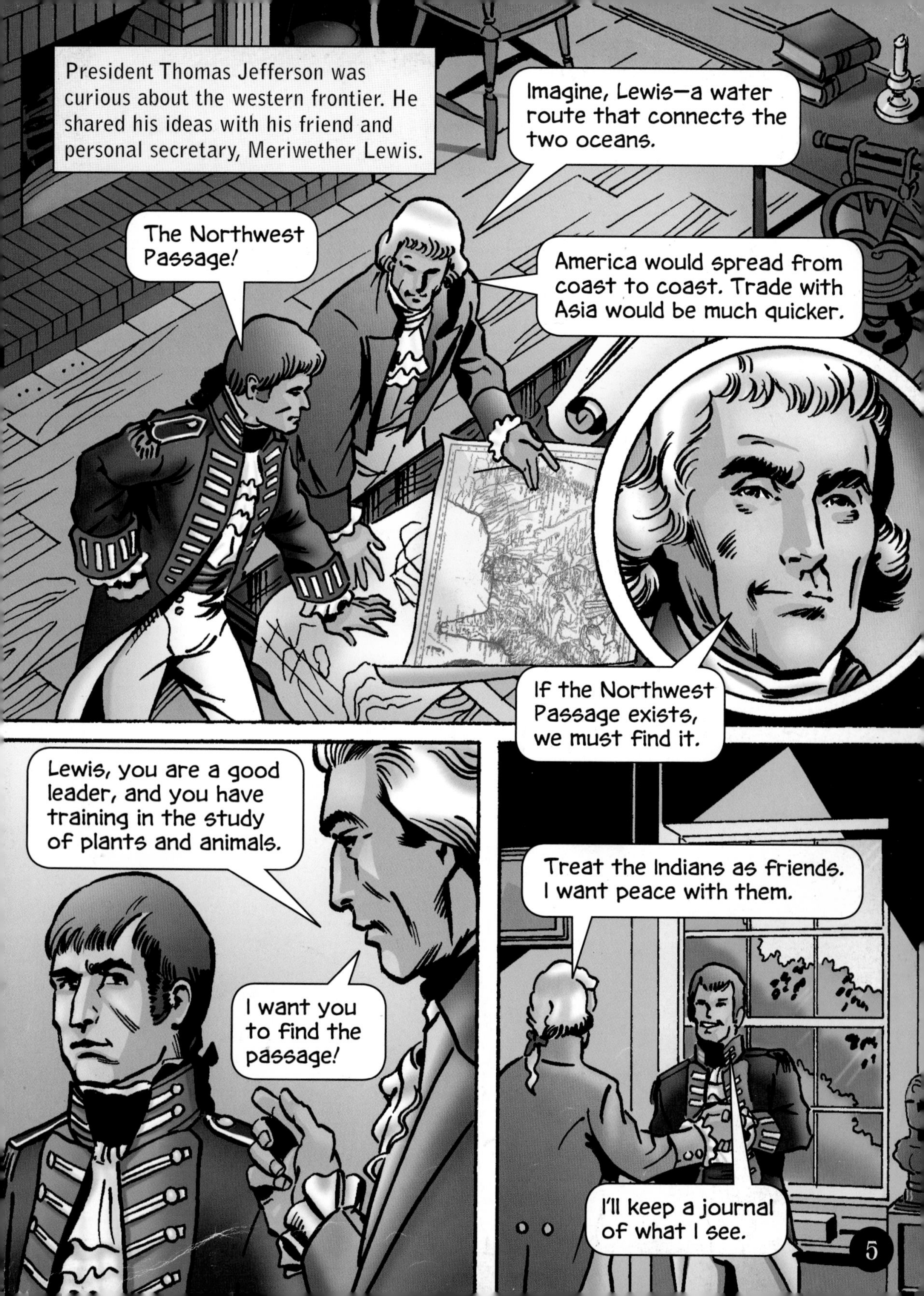
President Thomas Jefferson was curious about the western frontier. He shared his ideas with his friend and personal secretary, Meriwether Lewis.
Imagine, Lewis—a water route that connects the two oceans.
The Northwest Passage!
America would spread from coast to coast. Trade with Asia would be much quicker.
If the Northwest Passage exists, we must find it.
Lewis, you are a good leader, and you have training in the study of plants and animals.
I want you to find the passage!
Treat the Indians as friends. I want peace with them.
I'll keep a journal of what I see.

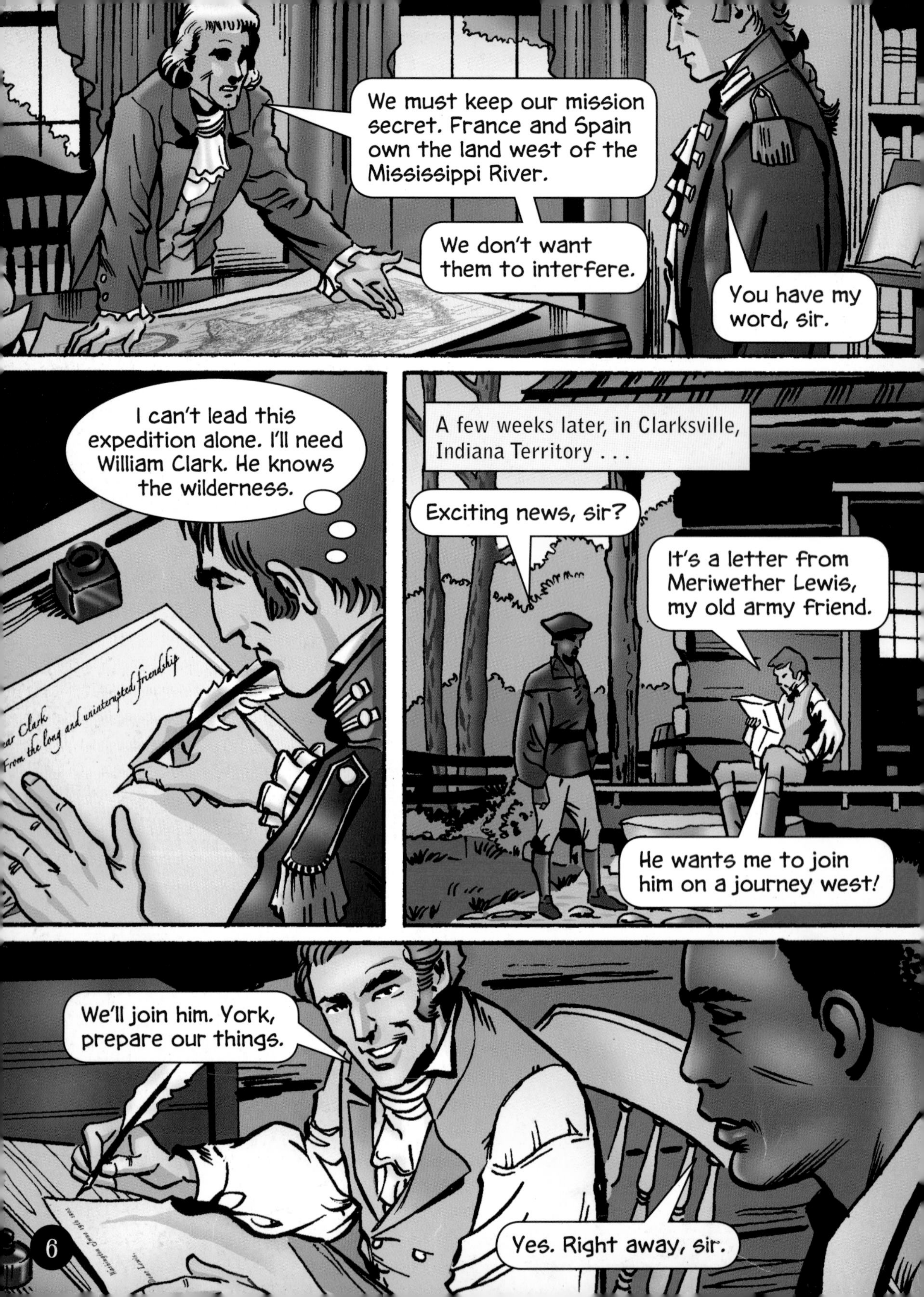

We must keep our mission secret. France and Spain own the land west of the Mississippi River.
We don't want them to interfere.
You have my word, sir.
I can't lead this expedition alone. I'll need William Clark. He knows the wilderness.
ear Clark
From the long and uninterrupted friendship
A few weeks later, in Clarksville, Indiana Territory . . .
Exciting news, sir?
It's a letter from Meriwether Lewis, my old army friend.
He wants me to join him on a journey west!
We'll join him. York, prepare our things.
Yes. Right away, sir.

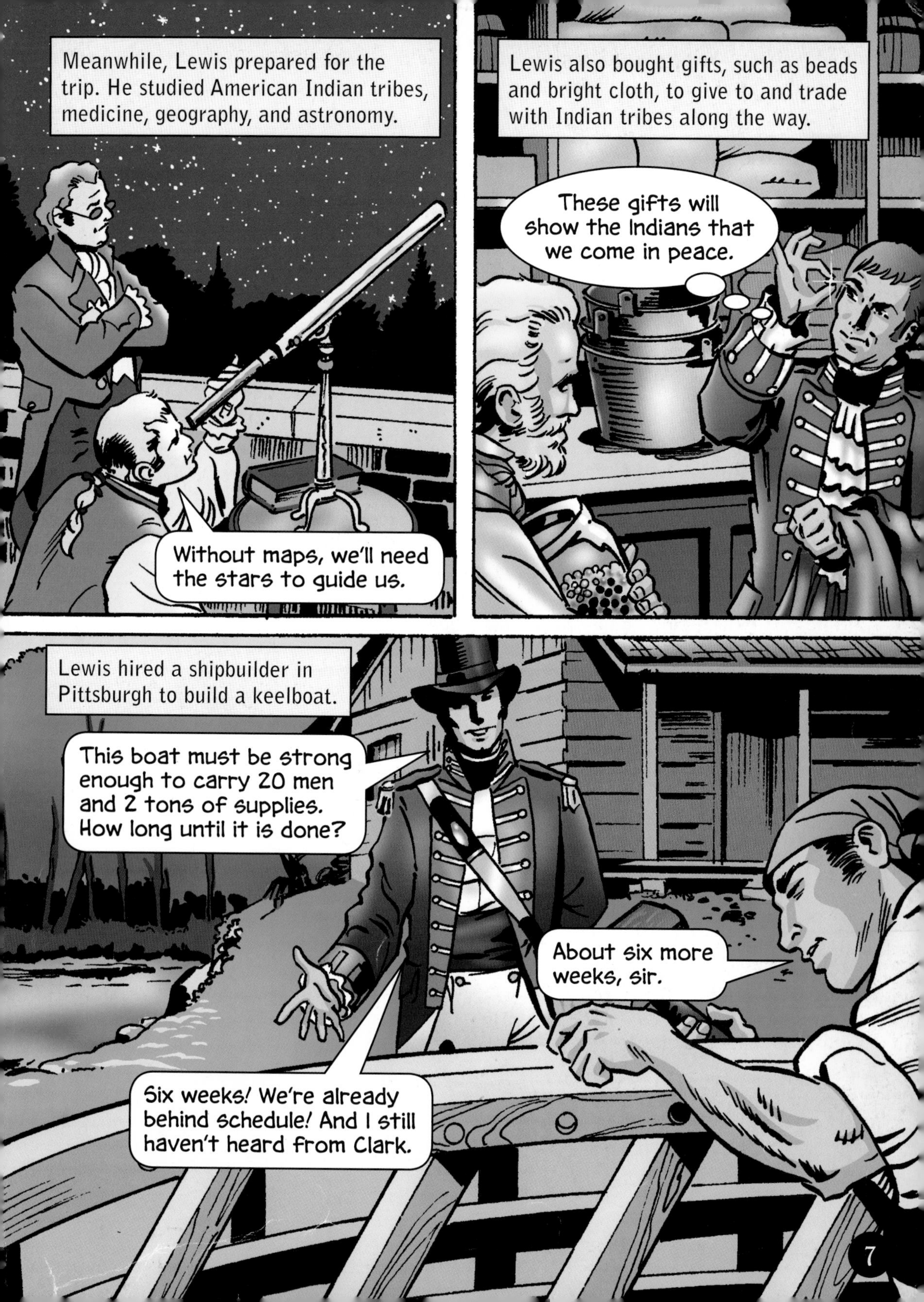

Meanwhile, Lewis prepared for the trip. He studied American Indian tribes, medicine, geography, and astronomy.
Without maps, we'll need the stars to guide us.
Lewis also bought gifts, such as beads and bright cloth, to give to and trade with Indian tribes along the way.
These gifts will show the Indians that we come in peace.
Lewis hired a shipbuilder in Pittsburgh to build a keelboat.
This boat must be strong enough to carry 20 men and 2 tons of supplies. How long until it is done?
About six more weeks, sir.
Six weeks! We're already behind schedule! And I still haven't heard from Clark.

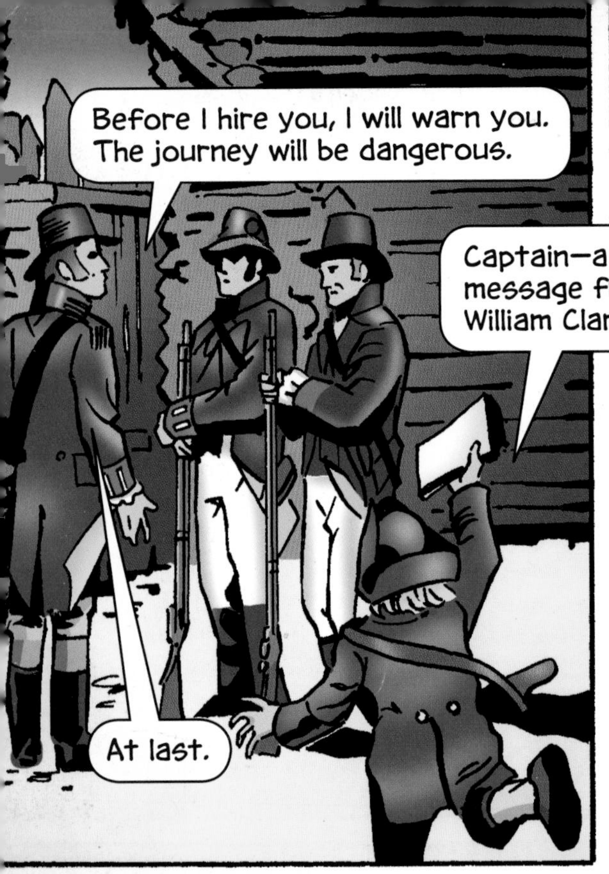
Before I hire you, I will warn you. The journey will be dangerous.
At last.
Captain—a message from William Clark!

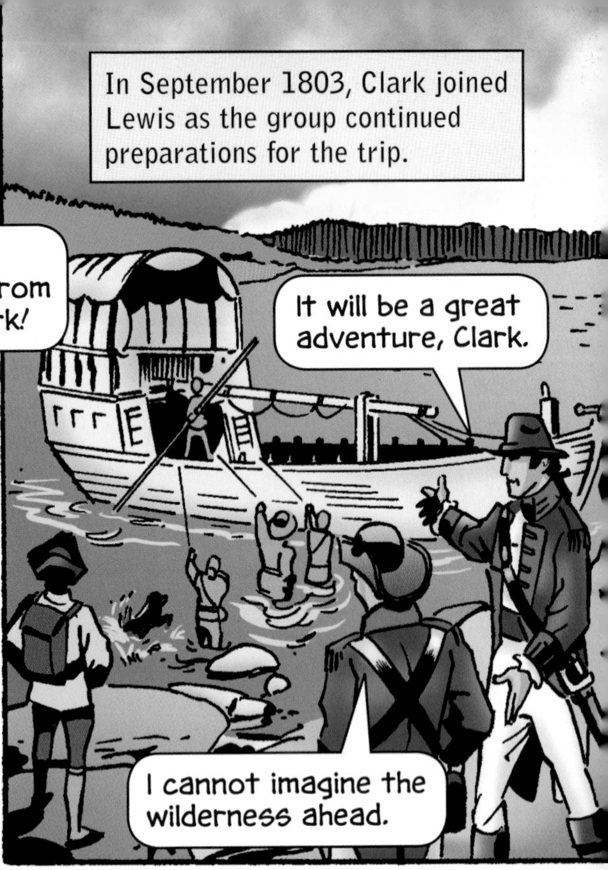
In September 1803, Clark joined Lewis as the group continued preparations for the trip.
It will be a great adventure, Clark.
I cannot imagine the wilderness ahead.

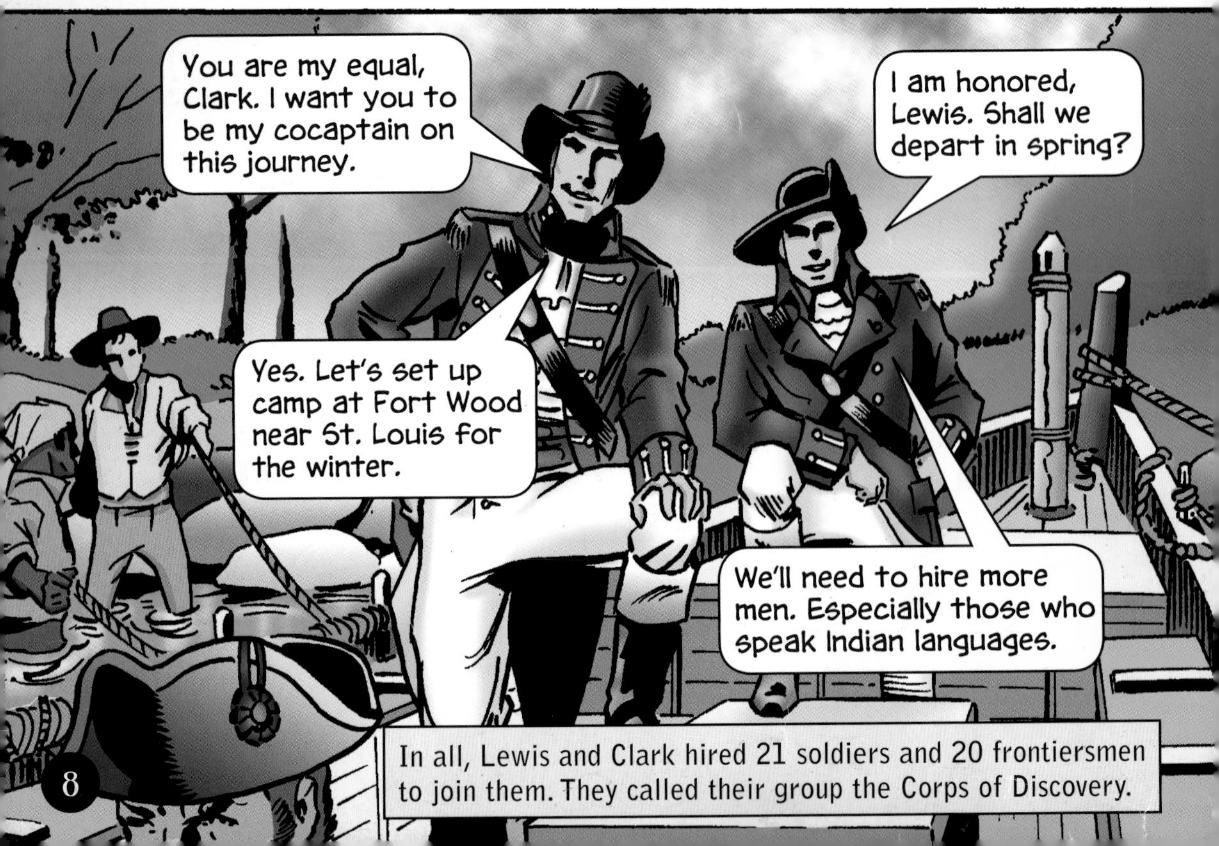
You are my equal, Clark. I want you to be my cocaptain on this journey.
I am honored, Lewis. Shall we depart in spring?
Yes. Let's set up camp at Fort Wood near St. Louis for the winter.
We'll need to hire more men. Especially those who speak Indian languages.
In all, Lewis and Clark hired 21 soldiers and 20 frontiersmen to join them. They called their group the Corps of Discovery.

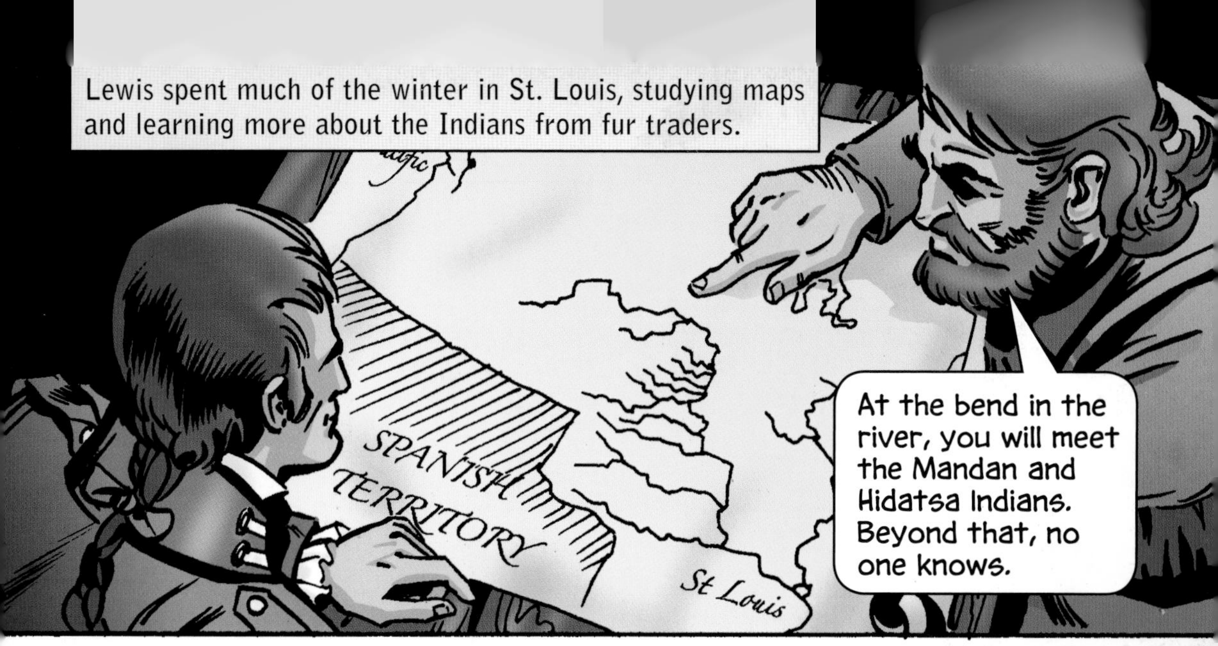
Lewis spent much of the winter in St. Louis, studying maps and learning more about the Indians from fur traders.
SPANISH TERRITORY
St Louis
At the bend in the river, you will meet the Mandan and Hidatsa Indians. Beyond that, no one knows.

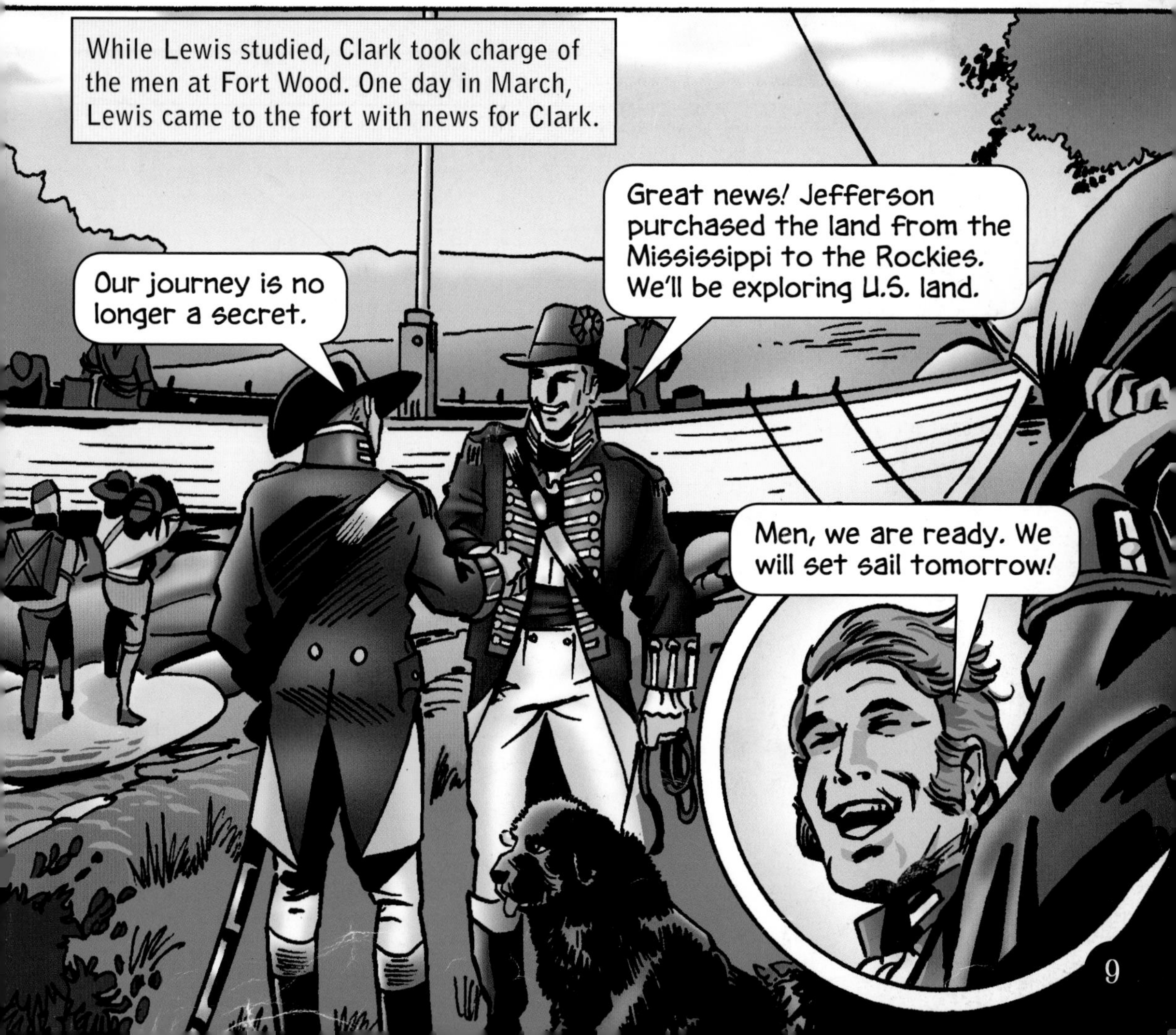
While Lewis studied, Clark took charge of the men at Fort Wood. One day in March, Lewis came to the fort with news for Clark.
Our journey is no longer a secret.
Great news! Jefferson purchased the land from the Mississippi to the Rockies. We'll be exploring U.S. land.
Men, we are ready. We will set sail tomorrow!

CHAPTER 2
INTO THE UNKNOWN

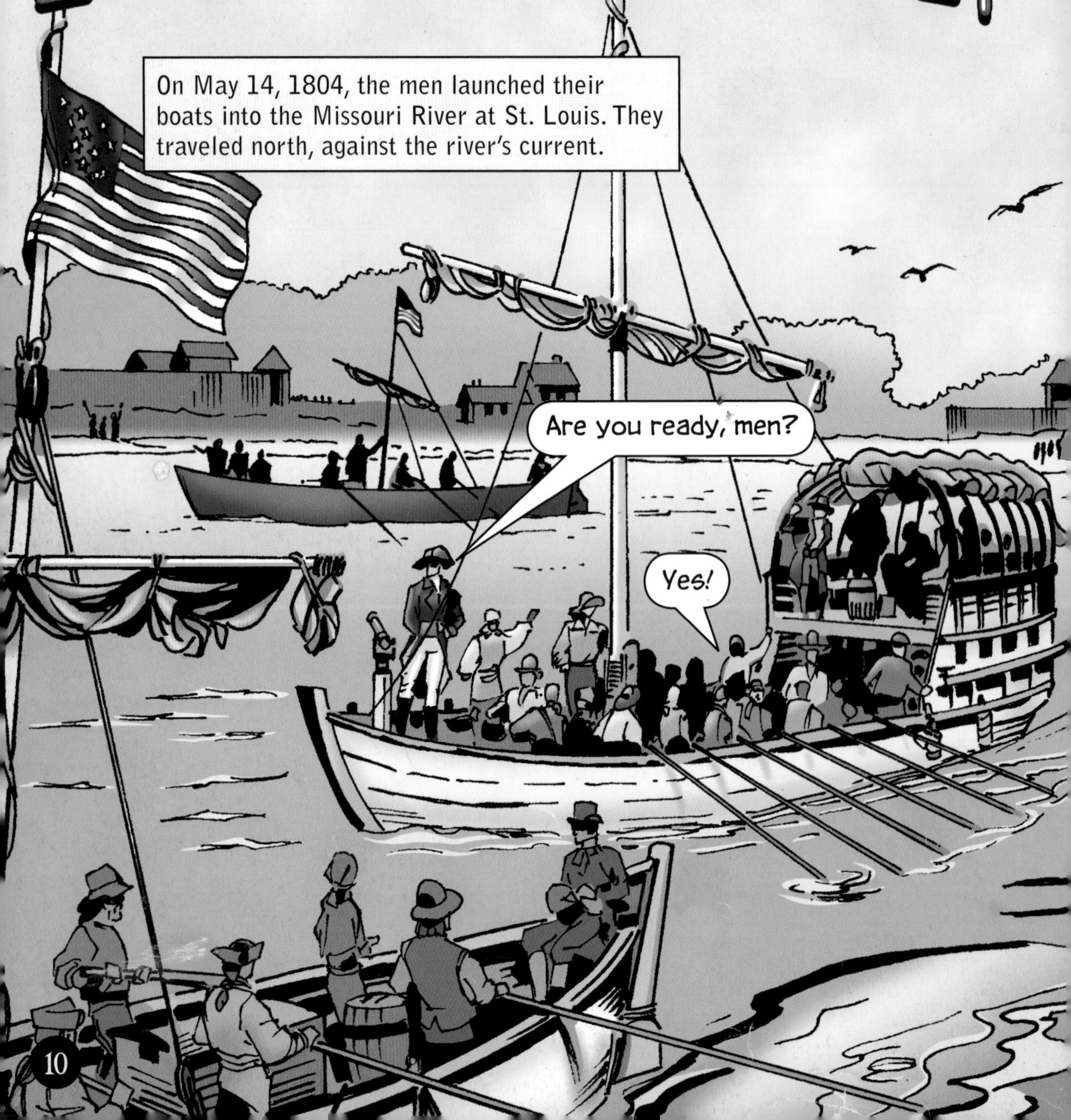

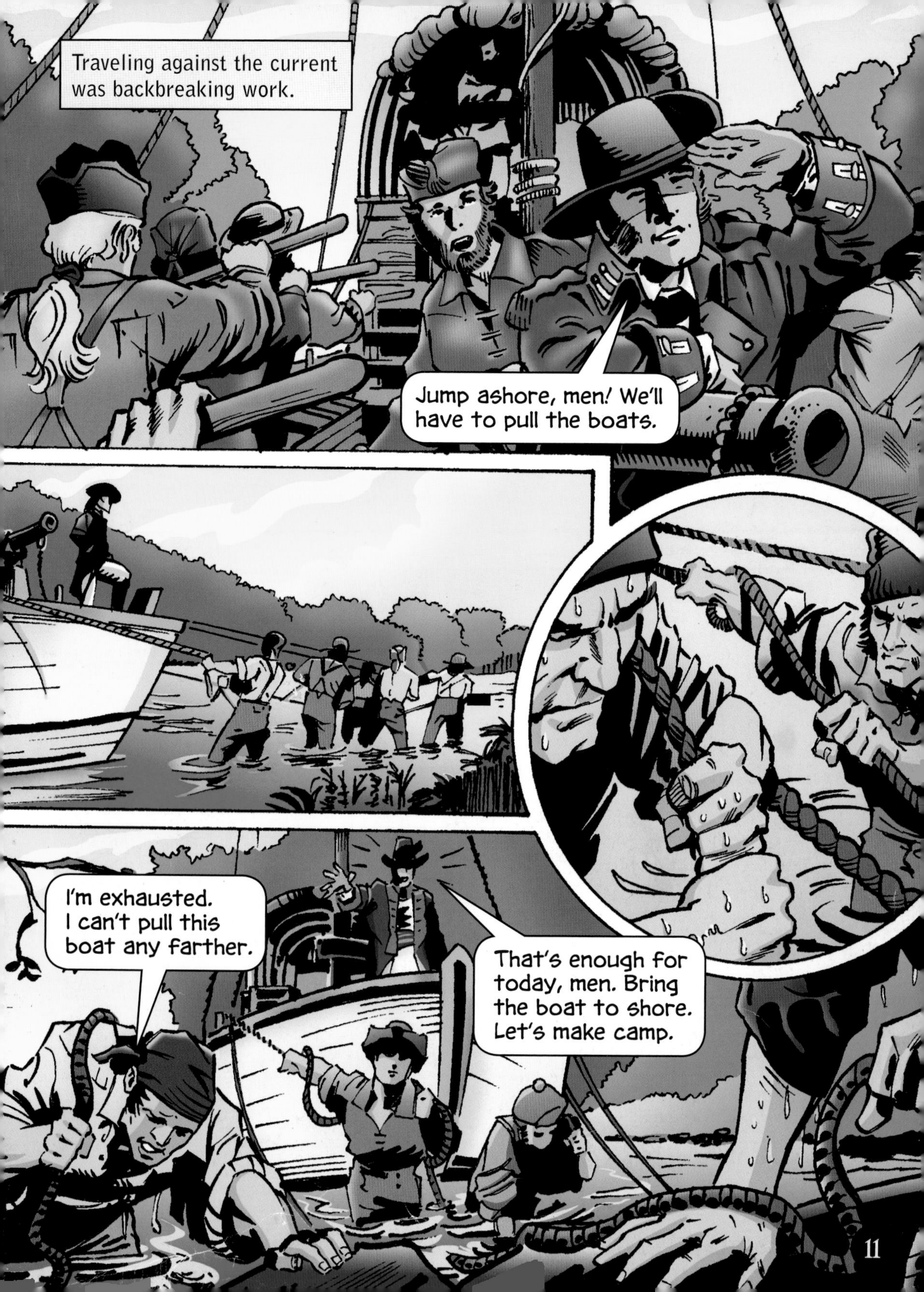
Traveling against the current was backbreaking work.
Jump ashore, men! We'll have to pull the boats.
I'm exhausted. I can't pull this boat any farther.
That's enough for today, men. Bring the boat to shore. Let's make camp.

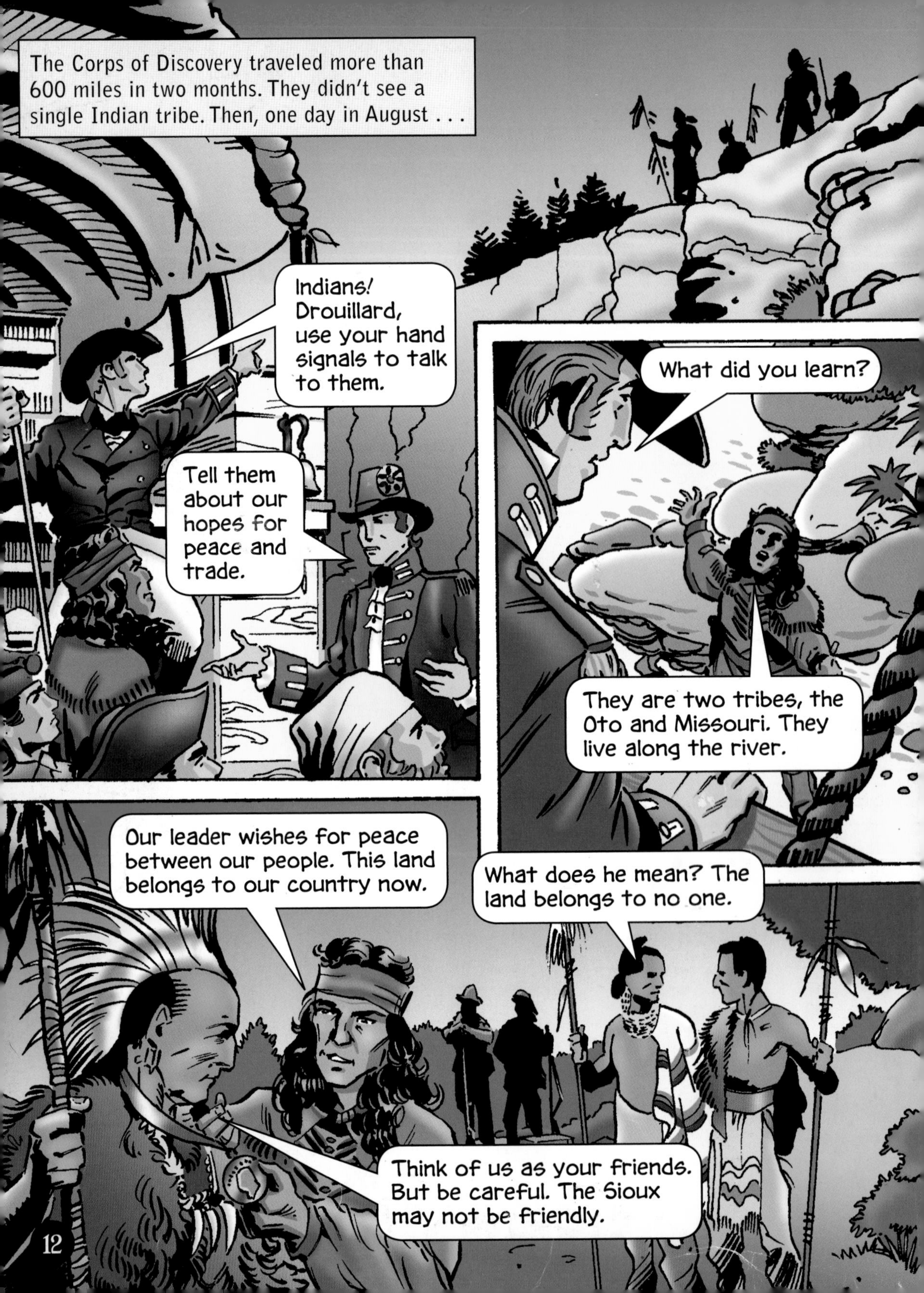
The Corps of Discovery traveled more than 600 miles in two months. They didn't see a single Indian tribe. Then, one day in August . . .
Indians! Drouillard, use your hand signals to talk to them.
Tell them about our hopes for peace and trade.
What did you learn?
They are two tribes, the Oto and Missouri. They live along the river.
Our leader wishes for peace between our people. This land belongs to our country now.
What does he mean? The land belongs to no one.
Think of us as your friends. But be careful. The Sioux may not be friendly.

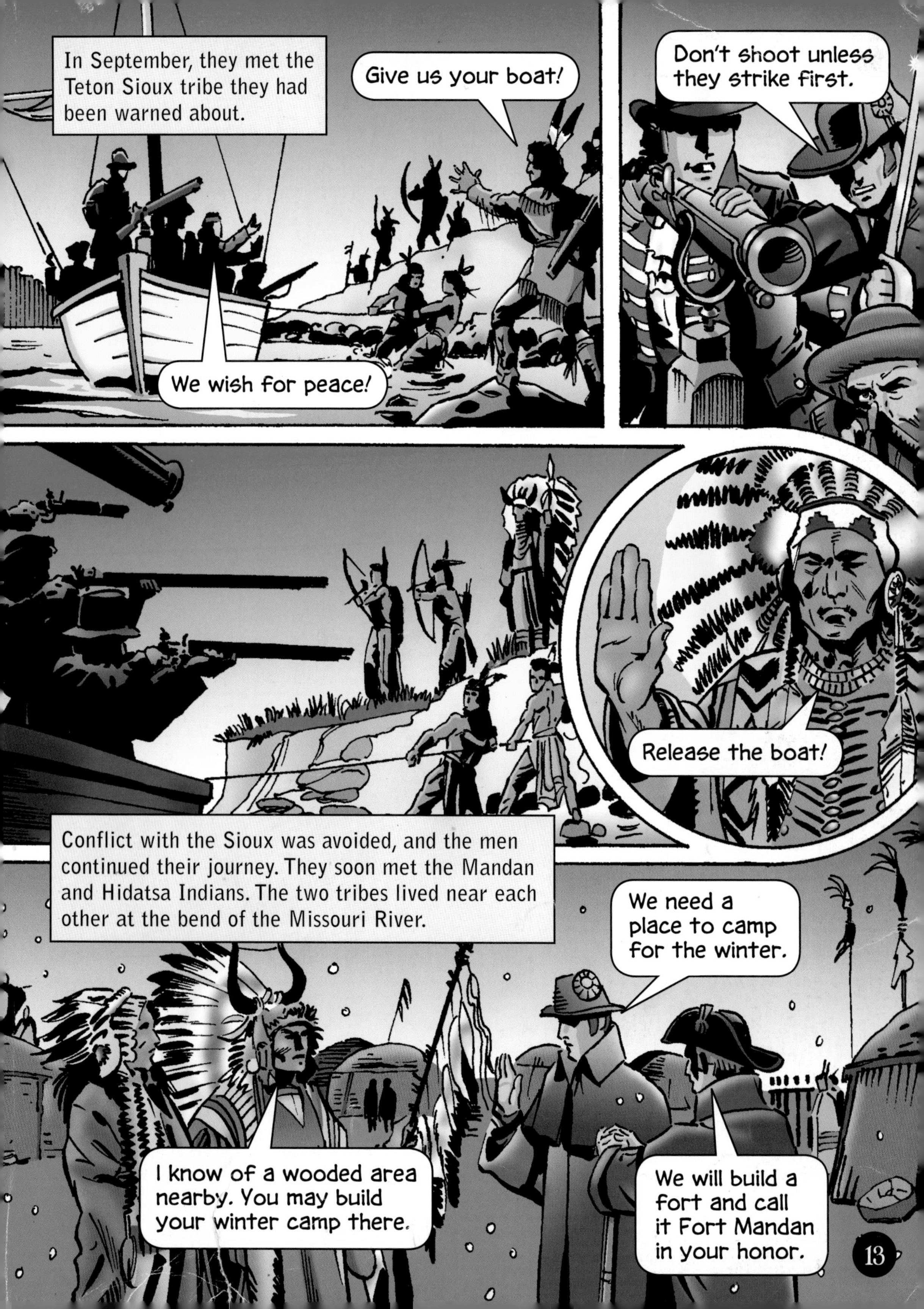
In September, they met the Teton Sioux tribe they had been warned about.
Give us your boat!
We wish for peace!
Don't shoot unless they strike first.
Release the boat!
Conflict with the Sioux was avoided, and the men continued their journey. They soon met the Mandan and Hidatsa Indians. The two tribes lived near each other at the bend of the Missouri River.
We need a place to camp for the winter.
I know of a wooded area nearby. You may build your winter camp there.
We will build a fort and call it Fort Mandan in your honor.

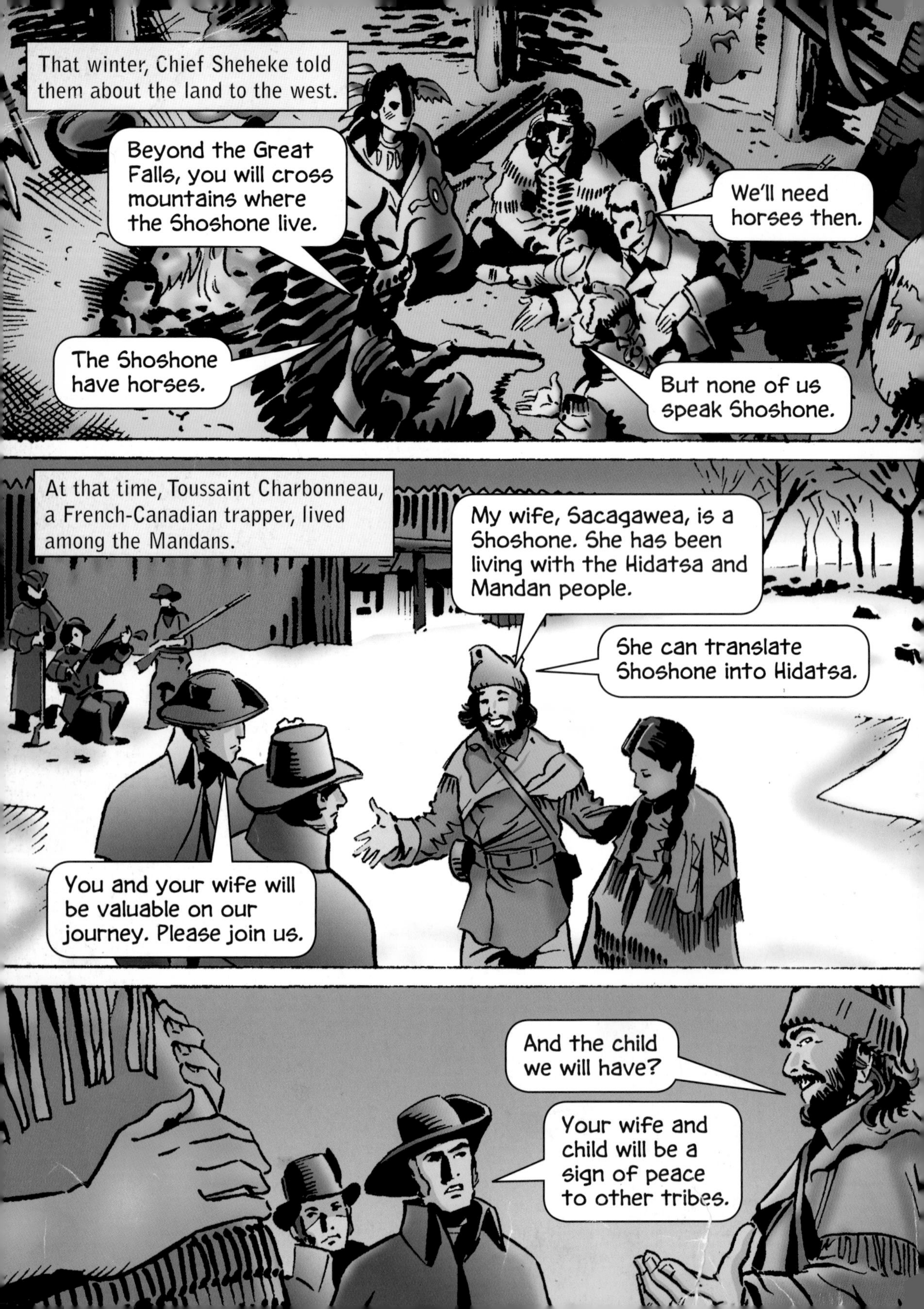

That winter, Chief Sheheke told them about the land to the west.
Beyond the Great Falls, you will cross mountains where the Shoshone live.
We'll need horses then.
The Shoshone have horses.
But none of us speak Shoshone.
At that time, Toussaint Charbonneau, a French-Canadian trapper, lived among the Mandans.
My wife, Sacagawea, is a Shoshone. She has been living with the Hidatsa and Mandan people.
She can translate Shoshone into Hidatsa.
You and your wife will be valuable on our journey. Please join us.
And the child we will have?
Your wife and child will be a sign of peace to other tribes.

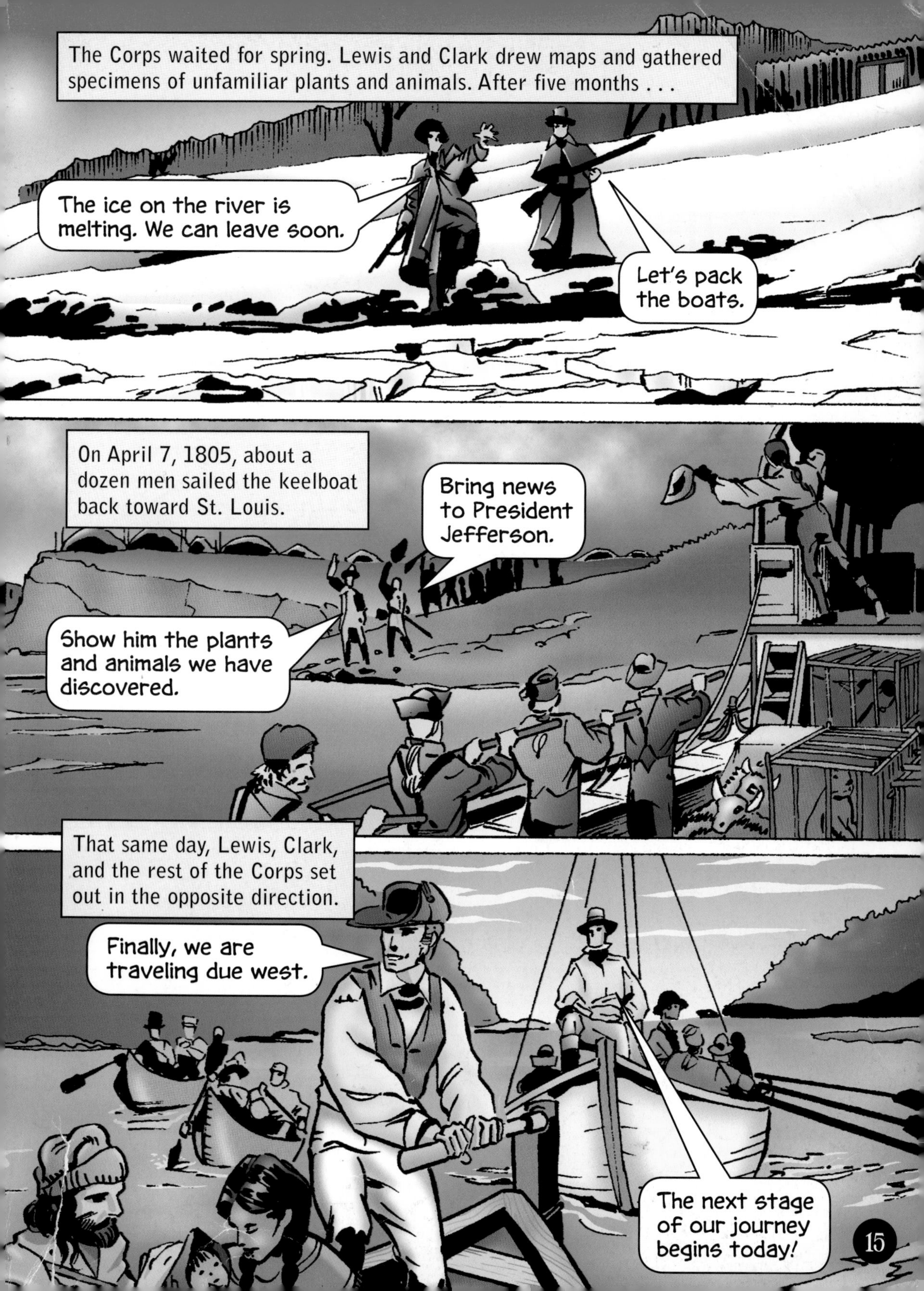
The Corps waited for spring. Lewis and Clark drew maps and gathered specimens of unfamiliar plants and animals. After five months . . .
The ice on the river is melting. We can leave soon.
Let's pack the boats.
On April 7, 1805, about a dozen men sailed the keelboat back toward St. Louis.
Bring news to President Jefferson.
Show him the plants and animals we have discovered.
That same day, Lewis, Clark, and the rest of the Corps set out in the opposite direction.
Finally, we are traveling due west.
The next stage of our journey begins today!

CHAPTER 3
OCEAN IN VIEW

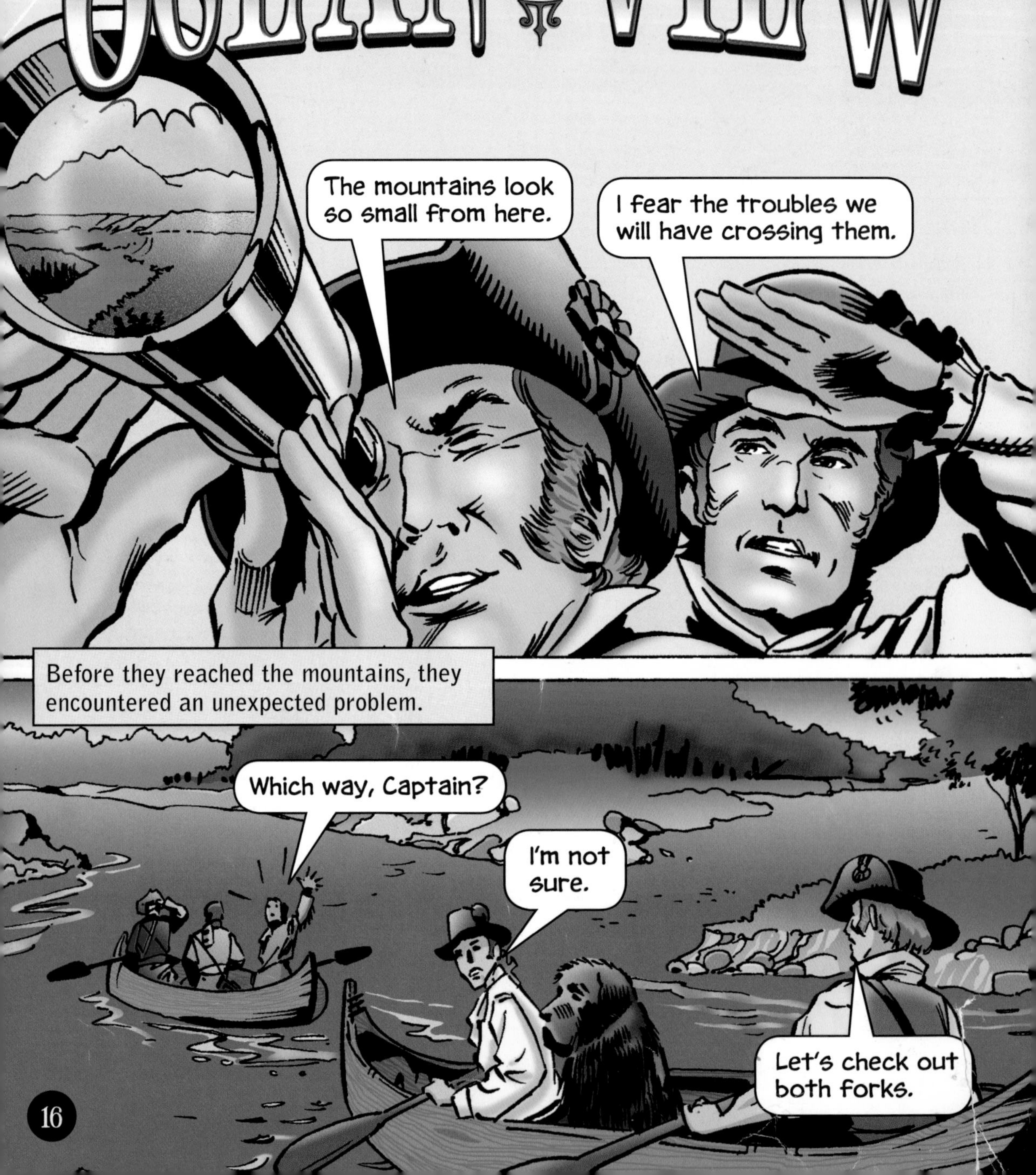
The mountains look so small from here.
I fear the troubles we will have crossing them.
Before they reached the mountains, they encountered an unexpected problem.
Which way, Captain?
I'm not sure.
Let's check out both forks.

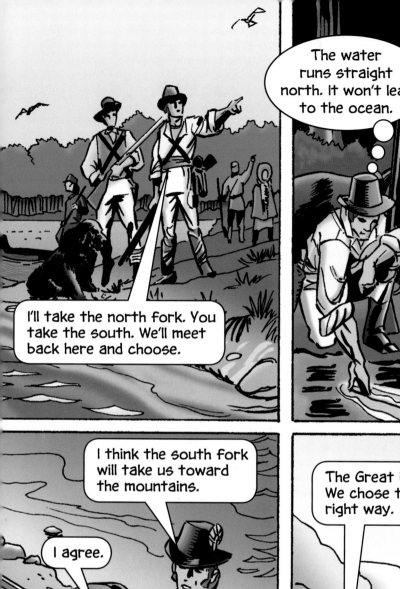

I'll take the north fork. You take the south. We'll meet back here and choose.

The water runs straight north. It won't lead to the ocean.

Clear, like mountain water.

I think the south fork will take us toward the mountains.

I agree.

Take the south fork, men!

If we're wrong, we'll be delayed for weeks.

The Great Falls! We chose the right way.

We'll have to carry everything around them.

It shouldn't take more than a few days.

17

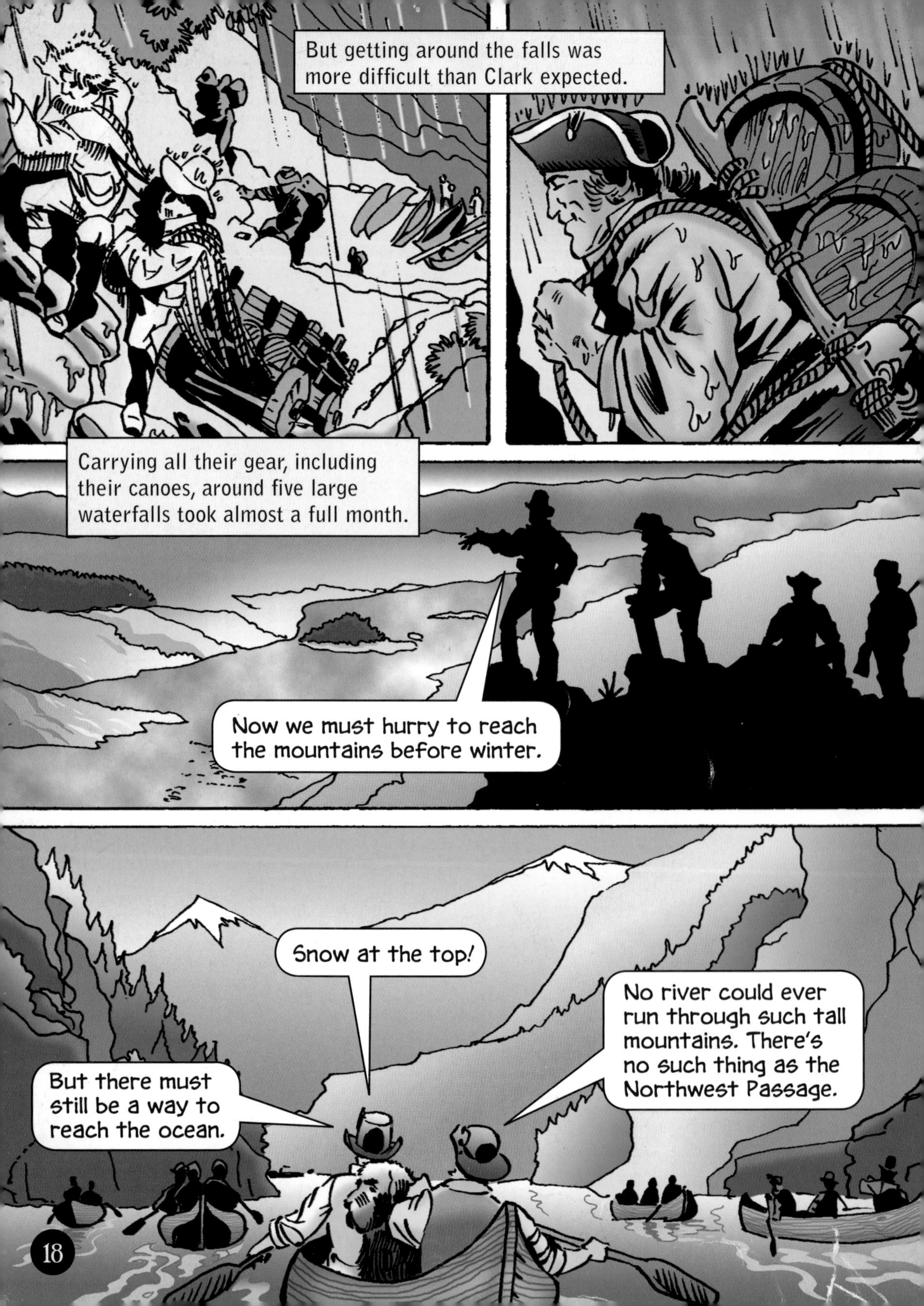

But getting around the falls was more difficult than Clark expected.
Carrying all their gear, including their canoes, around five large waterfalls took almost a full month.
Now we must hurry to reach the mountains before winter.
Snow at the top!
But there must still be a way to reach the ocean.
No river could ever run through such tall mountains. There's no such thing as the Northwest Passage.

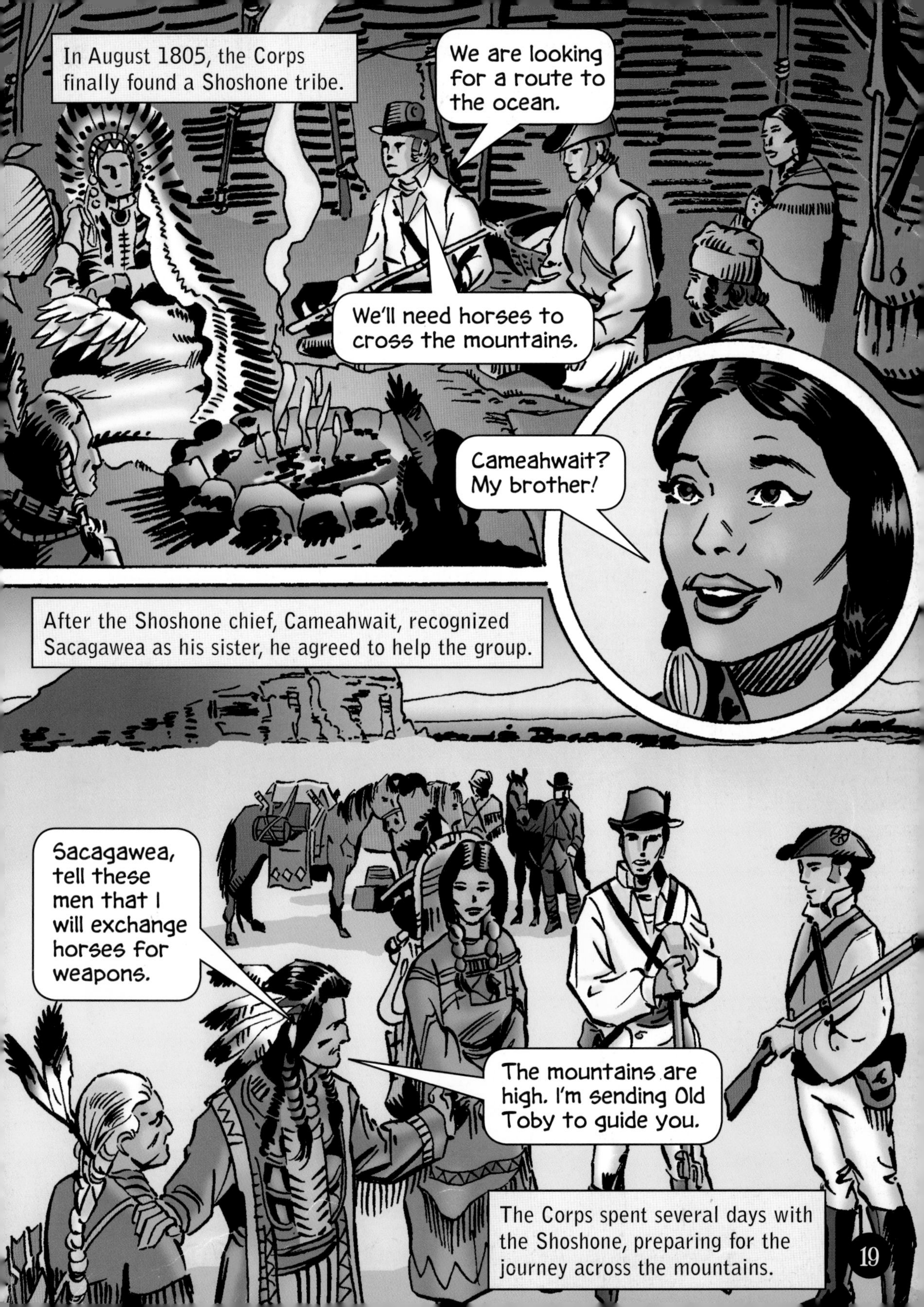
In August 1805, the Corps finally found a Shoshone tribe.
We are looking for a route to the ocean.
We'll need horses to cross the mountains.
Cameahwait? My brother!
After the Shoshone chief, Cameahwait, recognized Sacagawea as his sister, he agreed to help the group.
Sacagawea, tell these men that I will exchange horses for weapons.
The mountains are high. I'm sending Old Toby to guide you.
The Corps spent several days with the Shoshone, preparing for the journey across the mountains.

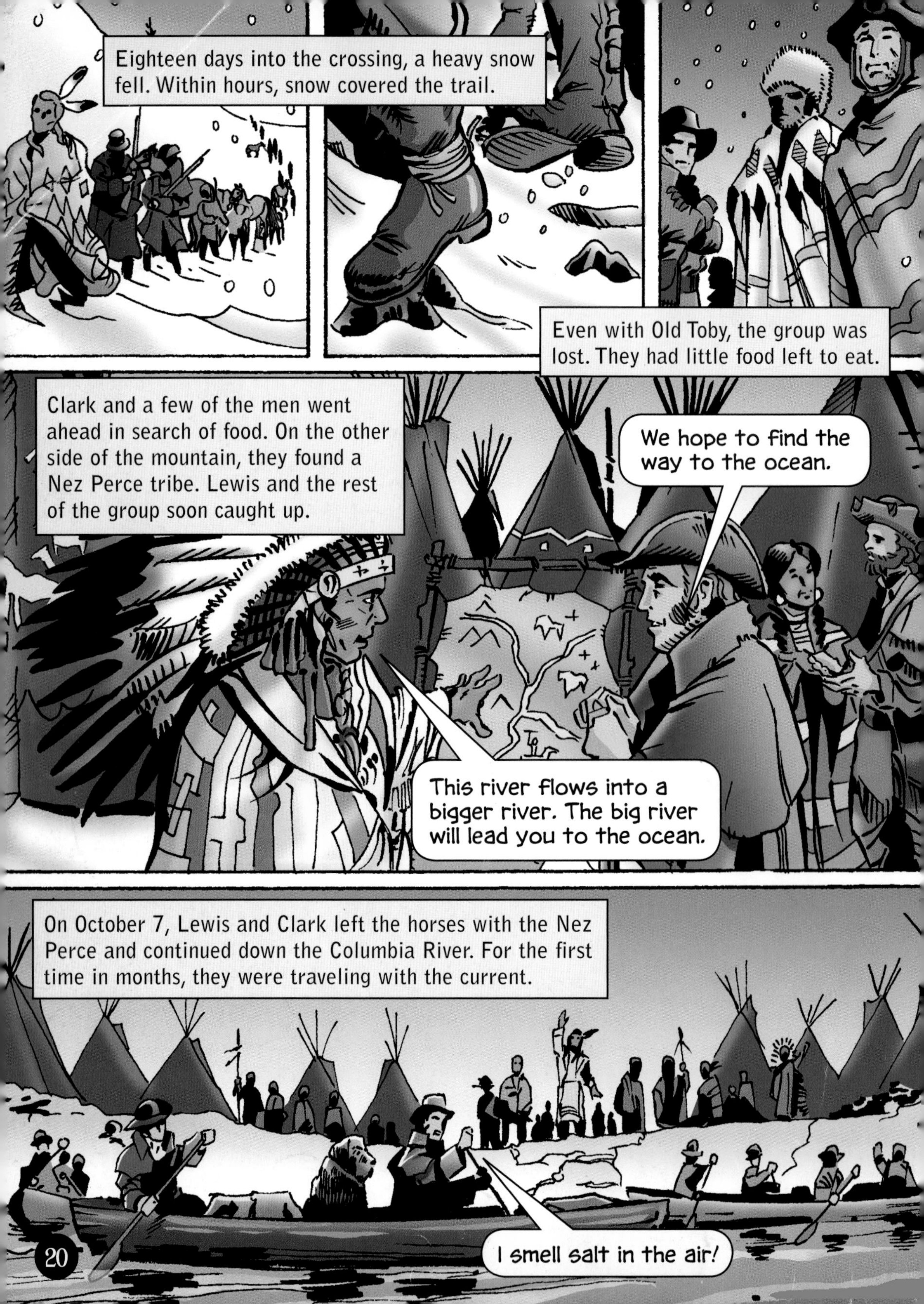
Eighteen days into the crossing, a heavy snow fell. Within hours, snow covered the trail.
Even with Old Toby, the group was lost. They had little food left to eat.
Clark and a few of the men went ahead in search of food. On the other side of the mountain, they found a Nez Perce tribe. Lewis and the rest of the group soon caught up.
We hope to find the way to the ocean.
This river flows into a bigger river. The big river will lead you to the ocean.
On October 7, Lewis and Clark left the horses with the Nez Perce and continued down the Columbia River. For the first time in months, they were traveling with the current.
I smell salt in the air!

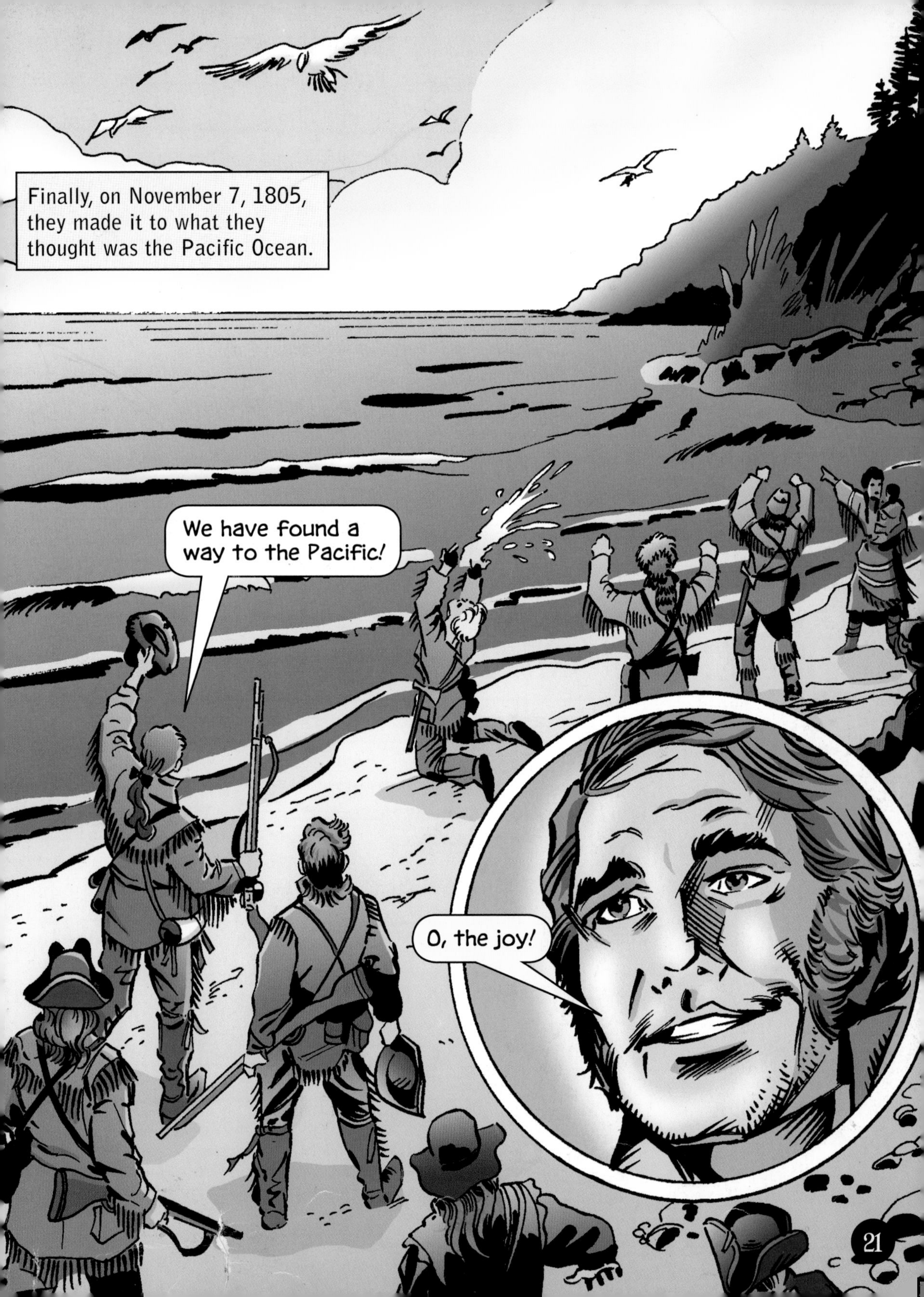
Finally, on November 7, 1805, they made it to what they thought was the Pacific Ocean.
We have found a way to the Pacific!
O, the joy!

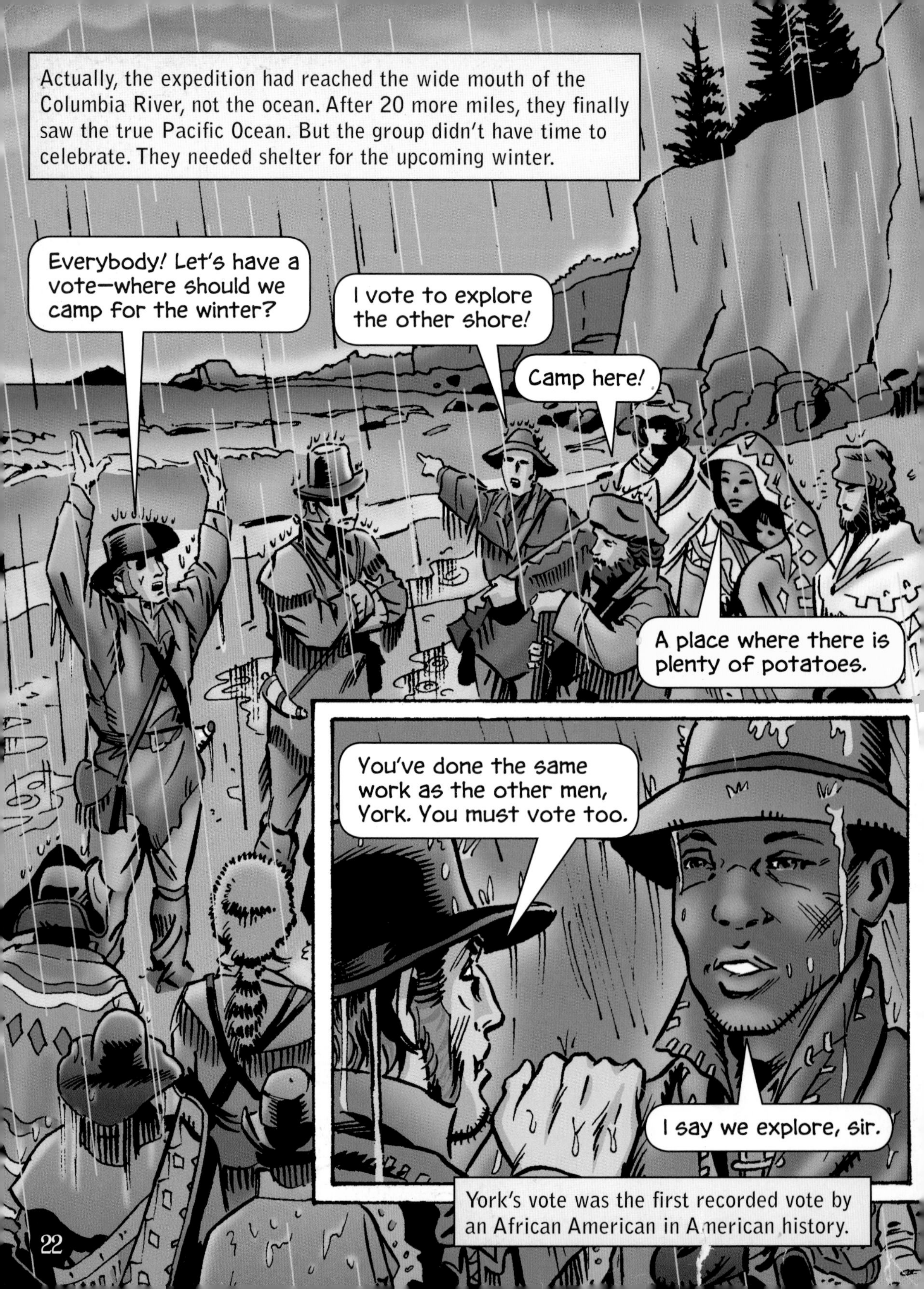
Actually, the expedition had reached the wide mouth of the Columbia River, not the ocean. After 20 more miles, they finally saw the true Pacific Ocean. But the group didn't have time to celebrate. They needed shelter for the upcoming winter.
Everybody! Let's have a vote—where should we camp for the winter?
I vote to explore the other shore!
Camp here!
A place where there is plenty of potatoes.
You've done the same work as the other men, York. You must vote too.
I say we explore, sir.
York's vote was the first recorded vote by an African American in American history.

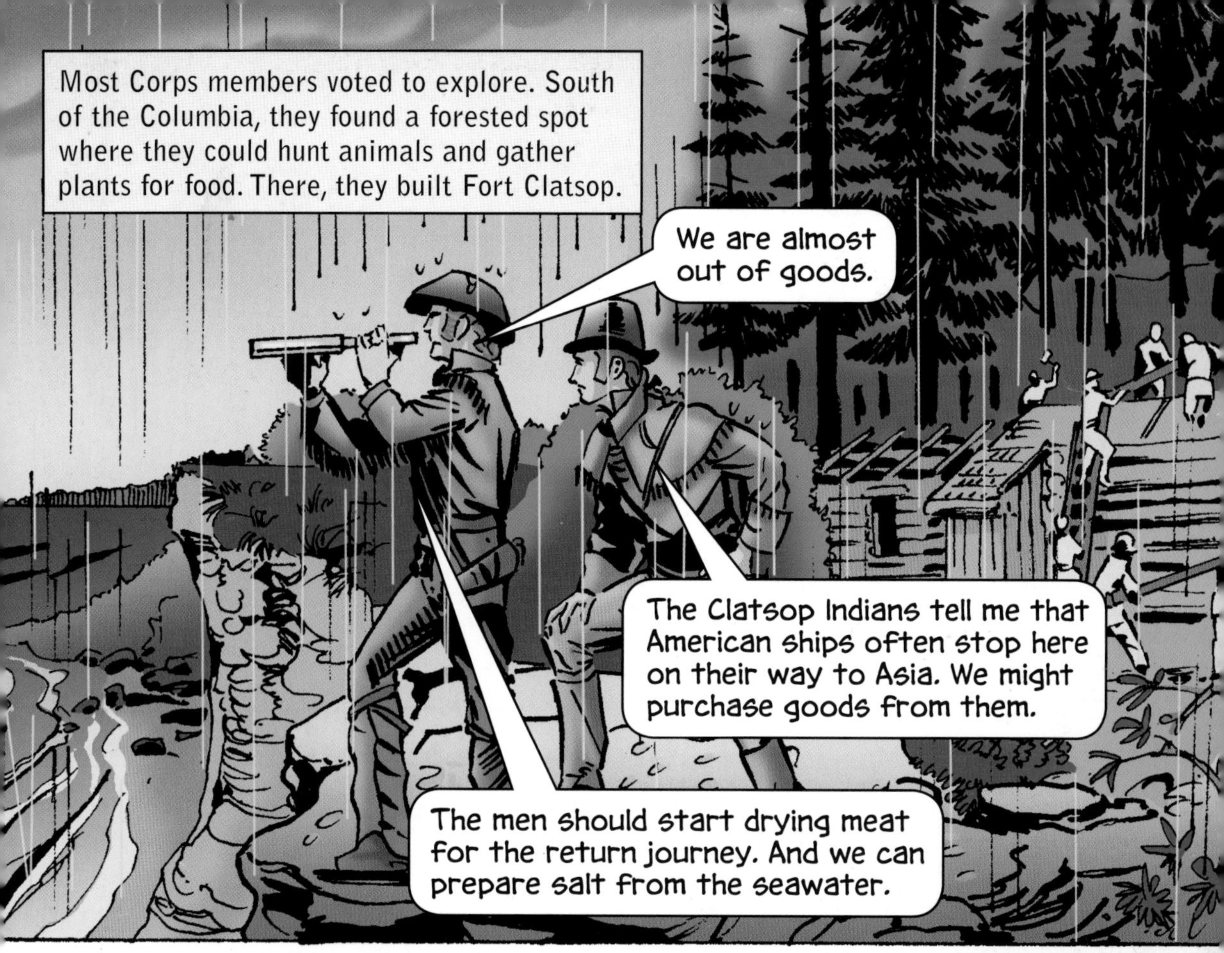
Most Corps members voted to explore. South of the Columbia, they found a forested spot where they could hunt animals and gather plants for food. There, they built Fort Clatsop.
We are almost out of goods.
The Clatsop Indians tell me that American ships often stop here on their way to Asia. We might purchase goods from them.
The men should start drying meat for the return journey. And we can prepare salt from the seawater.

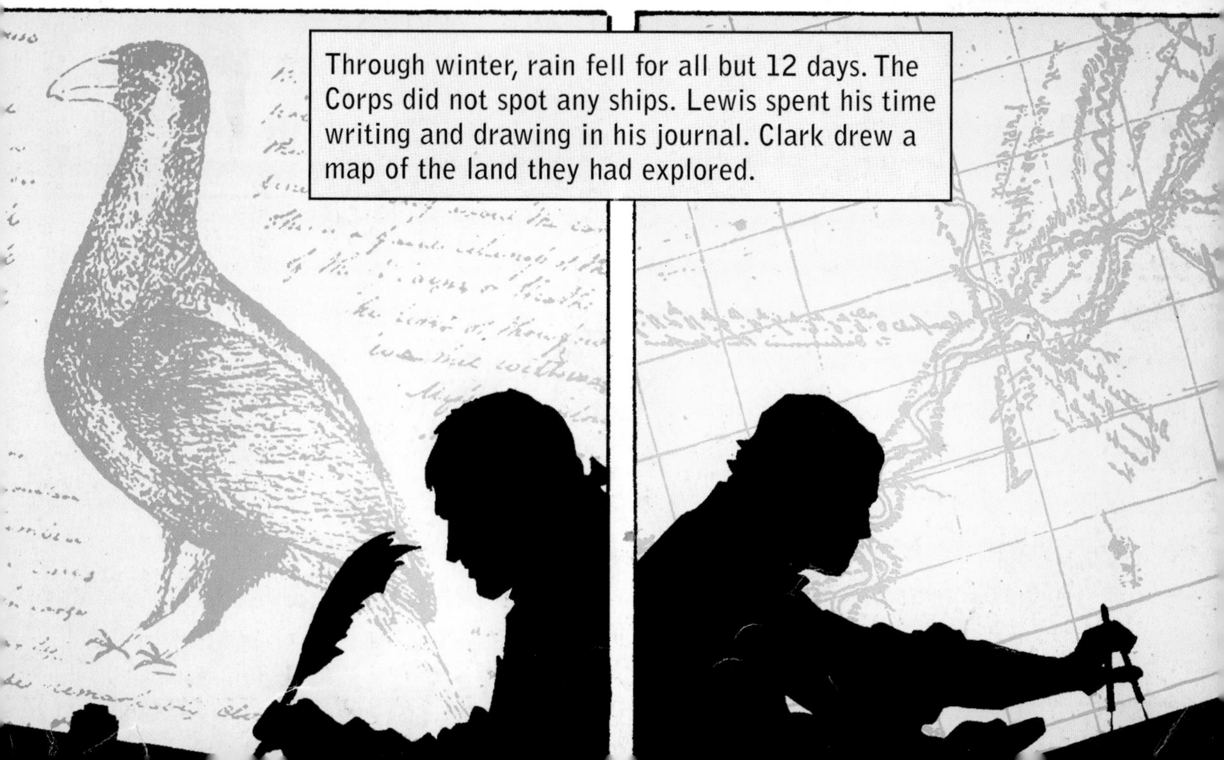
Through winter, rain fell for all but 12 days. The Corps did not spot any ships. Lewis spent his time writing and drawing in his journal. Clark drew a map of the land they had explored.

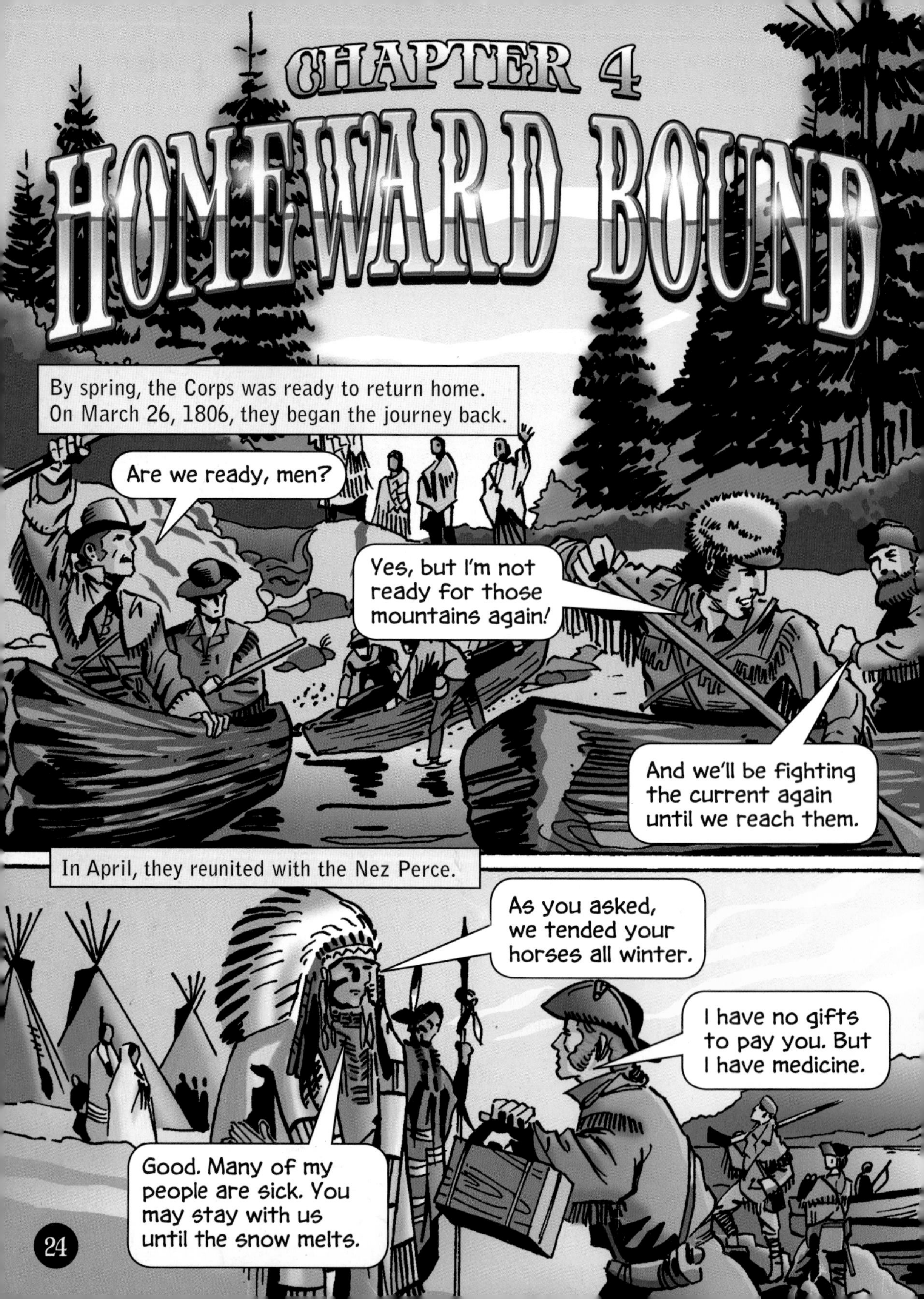
CHAPTER 4
HOMEWARD BOUND
By spring, the Corps was ready to return home. On March 26, 1806, they began the journey back.
Are we ready, men?
Yes, but I'm not ready for those mountains again!
And we'll be fighting the current again until we reach them.
In April, they reunited with the Nez Perce.
As you asked, we tended your horses all winter.
I have no gifts to pay you. But I have medicine.
Good. Many of my people are sick. You may stay with us until the snow melts.

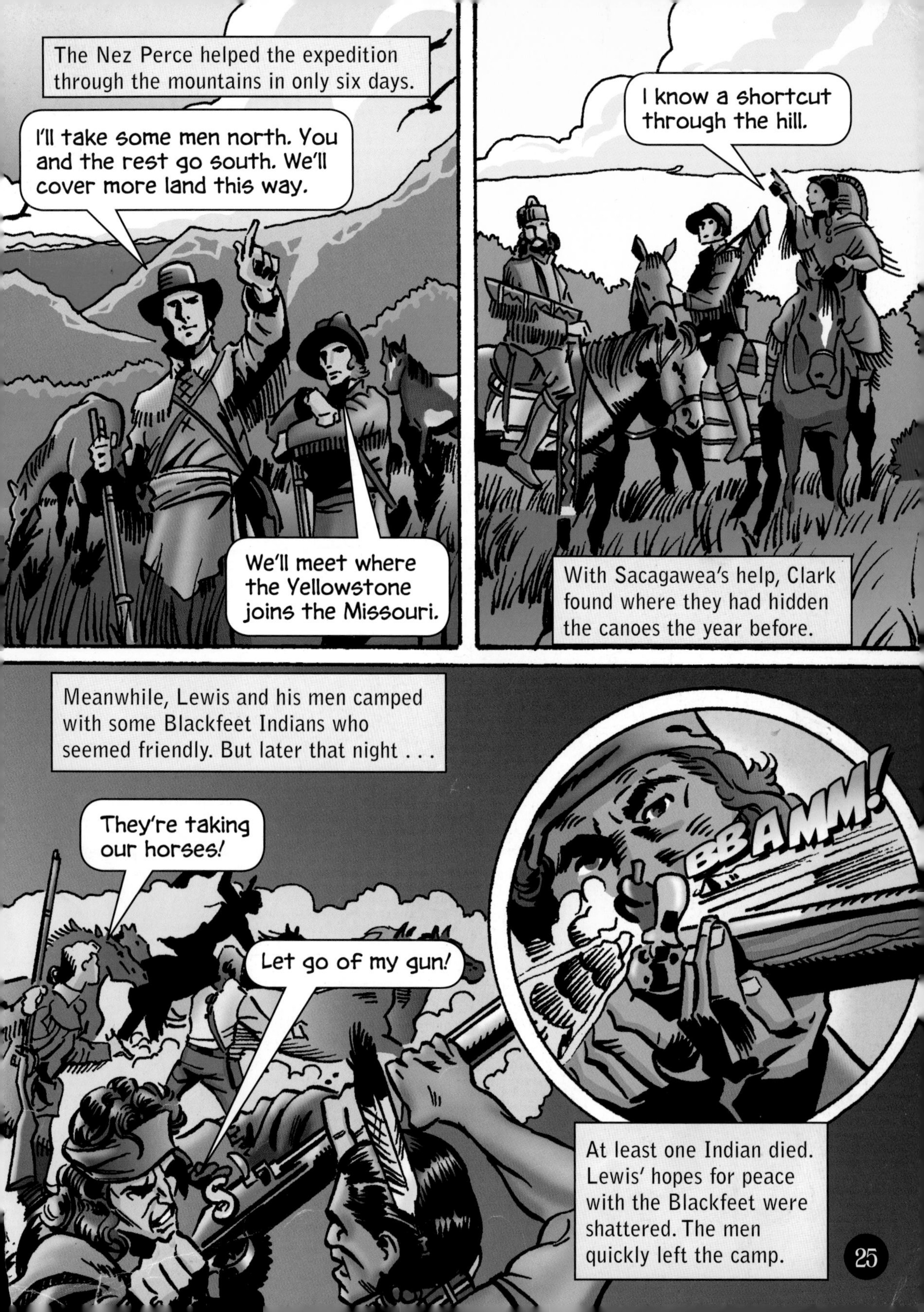
The Nez Perce helped the expedition through the mountains in only six days.
I'll take some men north. You and the rest go south. We'll cover more land this way.
We'll meet where the Yellowstone joins the Missouri.
I know a shortcut through the hill.
With Sacagawea's help, Clark found where they had hidden the canoes the year before.
Meanwhile, Lewis and his men camped with some Blackfeet Indians who seemed friendly. But later that night . . .
They're taking our horses!
Let go of my gun!
BBAMM!
At least one Indian died. Lewis' hopes for peace with the Blackfeet were shattered. The men quickly left the camp.

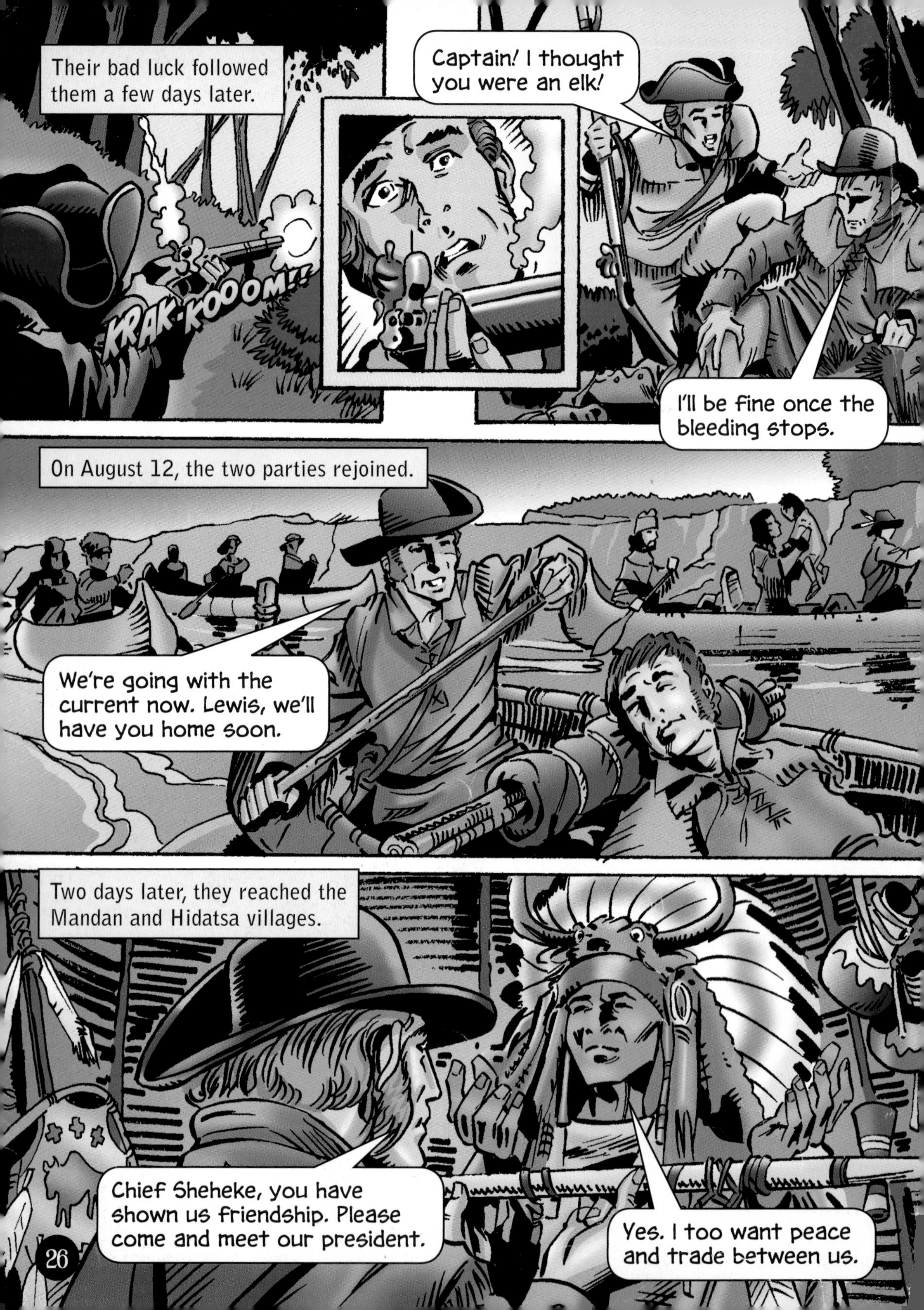
Their bad luck followed them a few days later.
KRAK-KOOOM!!
Captain! I thought you were an elk!
I'll be fine once the bleeding stops.
On August 12, the two parties rejoined.
We're going with the current now. Lewis, we'll have you home soon.
Two days later, they reached the Mandan and Hidatsa villages.
Chief Sheheke, you have shown us friendship. Please come and meet our president.
Yes. I too want peace and trade between us.

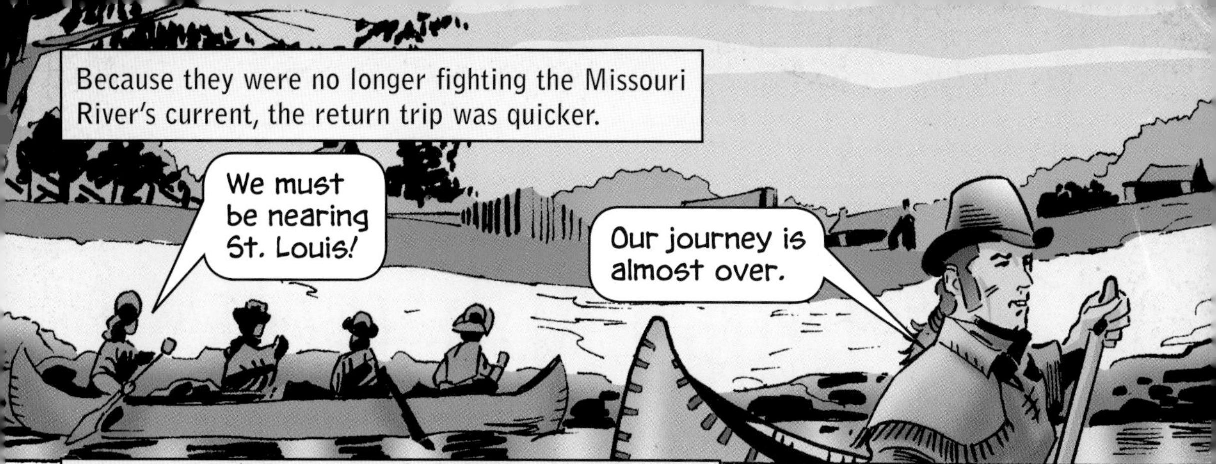
Because they were no longer fighting the Missouri River's current, the return trip was quicker.
We must be nearing St. Louis!
Our journey is almost over.

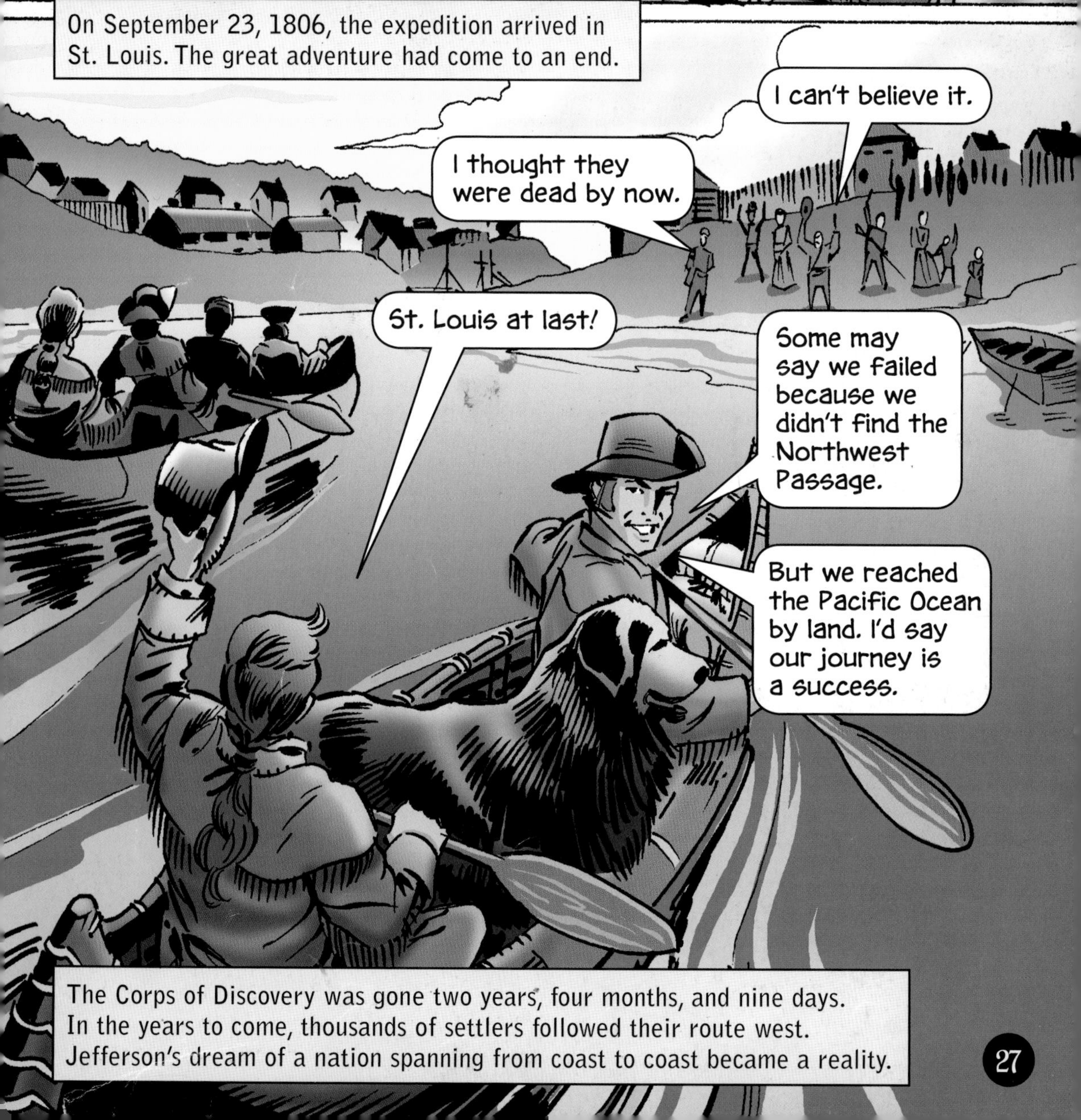
On September 23, 1806, the expedition arrived in St. Louis. The great adventure had come to an end.
I can't believe it.
I thought they were dead by now.
St. Louis at last!
Some may say we failed because we didn't find the Northwest Passage.
But we reached the Pacific Ocean by land. I'd say our journey is a success.
The Corps of Discovery was gone two years, four months, and nine days. In the years to come, thousands of settlers followed their route west. Jefferson's dream of a nation spanning from coast to coast became a reality.

MORE ABOUT THE EXPEDITION

⮞ Communication during the expedition was complicated. When possible, the Corps used the hand signals that were common among all tribes. At some villages, they found French traders who lived among the Indians and spoke their language. At the Shoshone villages, Lewis and Clark spoke English. A French-speaking Corps member translated the English to French. Charbonneau repeated it in Hidatsa. Sacagawea then spoke in Shoshone.

⮞ The explorers often had to eat whatever they could find. When they were nearly starving in the mountains, they ate horses and dogs. Throughout the journey, they ate beaver, squirrel, prairie dog, buffalo, whale, eagle, and swan. They also ate wild plants and roots.

⮞ Lewis and Clark discovered and described 122 species of animals, including the black-tailed prairie dog, grizzly bear, and harbor seal. Prickly pear cactus, bigleaf maple, and curlycup gumweed were among 178 species of plants that Lewis and Clark recorded for science for the first time.

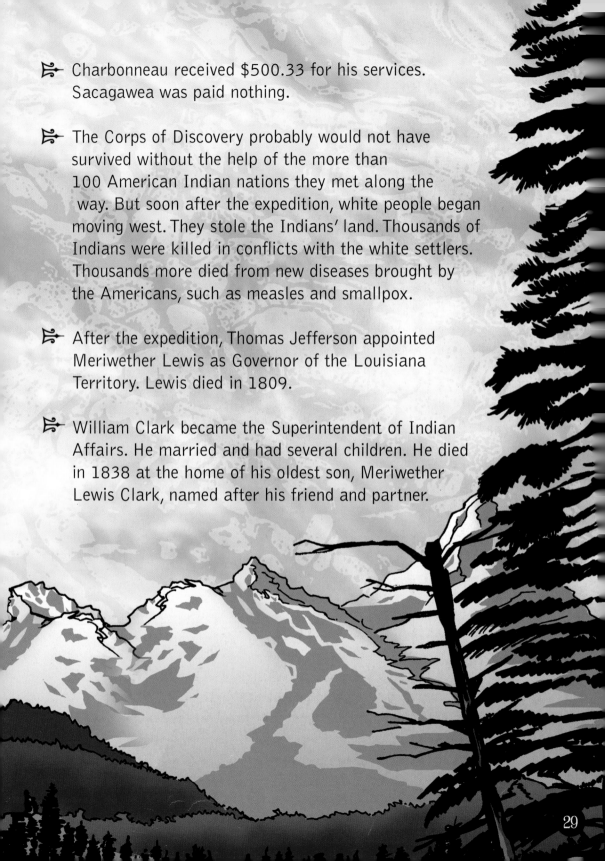

- Charbonneau received $500.33 for his services. Sacagawea was paid nothing.

- The Corps of Discovery probably would not have survived without the help of the more than 100 American Indian nations they met along the way. But soon after the expedition, white people began moving west. They stole the Indians' land. Thousands of Indians were killed in conflicts with the white settlers. Thousands more died from new diseases brought by the Americans, such as measles and smallpox.

- After the expedition, Thomas Jefferson appointed Meriwether Lewis as Governor of the Louisiana Territory. Lewis died in 1809.

- William Clark became the Superintendent of Indian Affairs. He married and had several children. He died in 1838 at the home of his oldest son, Meriwether Lewis Clark, named after his friend and partner.

GLOSSARY

astronomy (uh-STRON-uh-mee)—the study of stars, planets, and other objects in space

expedition (ek-spuh-DISH-uhn)—a long journey for a certain purpose, such as exploring

geography (jee-OG-ruh-fee)—the study of the earth's physical features

journal (JUR-nuhl)—a diary in which people regularly write down their thoughts and experiences

keelboat (KEEL-bote)—a type of riverboat that is usually rowed, poled, or towed and that is used for freight

specimen (SPESS-uh-muhn)—a sample or example used to stand for a whole group

INTERNET SITES

FactHound offers a safe, fun way to find Internet sites related to this book. All of the sites on FactHound have been researched by our staff.

Here's how:
1. Visit *www.facthound.com*
2. Choose your grade level.
3. Type in this book ID **0736864938** for age-appropriate sites. You may also browse subjects by clicking on letters, or by clicking on pictures and words.
4. Click on the **Fetch It** button.

FactHound will fetch the best sites for you!

READ MORE

Blumberg, Rhoda. *York's Adventures with Lewis and Clark: An African-American's Part in the Great Expedition.* New York: HarperCollins, 2004.

Fox, Michael D., and Suzanne G. *Meriwether Lewis and William Clark: The Corps of Discovery and the Exploration of the American Frontier.* New York: PowerPlus Books, 2005.

Gunderson, Jessica. *Sacagawea: Journey into the West.* Graphic Library: Graphic Biography. Mankato, Minn.: Capstone Press, 2007.

BIBLIOGRAPHY

DeVoto, Bernard, ed. *The Journals of Lewis and Clark.* Boston: Houghton Mifflin, 1953.

Jackson, Donald Dean, ed. *Letters of the Lewis and Clark Expedition, with Related Documents, 1783–1854.* Urbana, Ill.: University of Illinois Press, 1978.

MacGregor, Carol Lynn, ed. *The Journals of Patrick Gass: Member of the Lewis and Clark Expedition.* Missoula, Mont.: Mountain Press, 1997.

Moulton, Gary E., ed. *The Lewis and Clark Journals: An American Epic of Discovery: The Abridgment of the Definitive Nebraska Edition.* Lincoln, Neb.: University of Nebraska Press, 2003.

INDEX